George Sand, Charlotte C Johnston

The Master Mosaic-Workers

George Sand, Charlotte C Johnston

The Master Mosaic-Workers

ISBN/EAN: 9783337396633

Printed in Europe, USA, Canada, Australia, Japan

Cover: Foto ©Thomas Meinert / pixelio.de

More available books at **www.hansebooks.com**

THE
MASTER MOSAIC-WORKERS

BY

GEORGE SAND

TRANSLATED FROM THE FRENCH BY

CHARLOTTE C. JOHNSTON

BOSTON
LITTLE, BROWN, AND COMPANY
1895

THE MASTER MOSAIC-WORKERS.

INTRODUCTION.

WHILE it is true that the gifted author of "Consuelo" has not, in this charming novelette, adhered with absolute accuracy to known facts concerning the Venetian painters and mosaic-workers whom she introduces to her readers, she has followed them with sufficient closeness to justify the classification of the story as an historical romance.

Byzantine workers in mosaics found employment in Venice early in the history of Venetian civilization; and as the demand for work of this description increased, it was deemed advisable to form a school in which apprentices should be instructed in the art of setting colored stones in patterns on the walls of churches and other edifices to which this form of ornamentation was best adapted. About 1520 it seemed necessary to found a special establishment of professional workers in mosaics, assisted by designers selected from among the more eminent masters of the day, with especial reference to the restoration and renovation of the Cathedral of Saint Mark.

The founders of the modern school of mosaic artists were Marco Rizzo and Vincenzo Bianchini, who were appointed by the Senate in 1517. In 1524 an important addition was made to the school in the person of Francesco Zuccato, who for more than half a century remained the favorite and best-paid master of the Venetian government. In 1542 Bartolommeo Bozza became a pupil and assistant of Francesco.

Francesco and Valerio Zuccato were the sons of Sebastiano Zuccato, who was Titian's first master in the art of painting. All authors who have written upon the subject agree in ascribing much of the perfection attained in the mosaic art to the influence and encouragement of Titian, to whom the Zuccati were endeared by his early association with their father. Francesco's portrait was frequently painted by him.

The feud between the Zuccati and the Bianchini

eventually involved the friends and enemies of both families. It is said that Vincenzo Bianchini's imprisonment for coining was upon a charge made by Francesco.

The controversy which forms the main theme of this sketch seems to have arisen while Francesco and Valerio were employed upon the vestibule of Saint Mark, and the Bianchini were designing the tree of Jesse in the chapel of Sant' Isidore. The barbarism of writing *Saxibus* for *Saxis* was committed by Francesco himself, instead of by the procurator, and he remedied the error by the use of a piece of painted paper. " Bianchini received intelligence of this and other alleged irregularities from Bozza, who abandoned his master and went over to Bianchini, on grounds of which there is at present no explanation, and the *Procurator-Cassiere*, Melchior Michelle, was privately informed that irregularities had taken place which ought to be prevented or punished. A commission of inquiry was appointed, and the Procurator was present when the mosaics of the vestibule were washed, and the paper which covered *Saxibus* was swept away. On the 22d of May, 1563, after suspicion had been thus aroused, Melchior Michelle went to the cathedral, accompanied by Sansovino and followed by Titian, Jacopo Pistoja,

THE MASTER MOSAIC-WORKERS.

Andrea Schiavone, Jacopo Tintoretto, and Paolo Veronese, when a diligent examination of all the mosaics was made. It was found that paint had been used in various places; but the judges were unanimous in thinking that this was not material, as the mosaics were otherwise perfect. Still Francesco was ordered to renew the parts that had been painted, at his own expense; and Valerio was deprived of his salary till such time as he should prove his skill afresh."[1]

The following, from a contemporary source, throws a still stronger light upon the author's fidelity to history as the groundwork of her story.

"I must not here omit to mention," says Vasari in his Life of Titian, "that the art of mosaic, almost abandoned in all other places, is encouraged and kept in life by the Most Serene Senate of Venice, and of this Titian has been the principal cause; seeing that, so far as in him lies, he has ever labored to promote the exercise thereof, and to procure respectable remuneration for those who practise the art. All that has been done in Venice has been executed after the designs of Titian and

[1] Crowe and Cavalcaselle, "Life and Times of Titian."

other excellent painters, who have made colored cartoons for the same; thus the works are brought to perfection, as may be seen in the portico of San Marco, where there is a 'Judgment of Solomon,' so beautiful that it could scarcely be executed more delicately with the pencil and colors.[1] But in the art of mosaic there are none who have distinguished themselves more highly in our times than have Valerio and Vincenzio Zuccheri, natives of Treviso,[2] many stories by whom may be seen in San Marco. Those from the Apocalypse may more particularly be specified. In this work the four Evangelists, under the form of various animals, are seen to surround the throne of God; the Seven Candlesticks, and other things, are also represented so admirably well that to him who looks at them from below they appear to be paintings in oil. There are besides numerous small pictures by those artists, and these are filled with figures which look, I do not say like paintings only, but like miniatures; and yet they are made of stones joined together. There are portraits, moreover, of various person-

[1] The Judgment of Solomon is by Vincenzo Bianchini.
[2] According to Federici, these brothers, more correctly called Zuccati, were not of Treviso, but Da Ponta; and the name of the one was not Vincenzio, but Francesco.

ages, ... all executed so carefully, and with so much harmony, so admirable a distribution of light and shadow, and such exquisite tints of the carnations (to say nothing of other qualities), that no better or more perfect works of the kind could possibly be conceived. Bartolommeo Bozza has also worked on the Church of San Marco; he is the rival of the Zuccheri, and has acquitted himself in a sufficiently praiseworthy manner. But that which has most effectually contributed to the success of all these artists has without doubt been the superintendence of Titian, with the designs prepared for these mosaics by his hand."

There seems to be no historical foundation for the competition described in the later chapters, in which each competitor was required to produce a Saint Jerome in mosaic work, and which resulted in the rehabilitation of the Zuccati; but a Saint Jerome (or Girolamo) in mosaic by Francesco is known to have been presented to the Court of Savoy.

Upon the facts here sketched, the author has constructed a romance in no way unworthy of her enduring reputation. Not only by the lifelike glimpses it affords us of the great masters, at whose feet have sat so many generations of artists, nor

by its vivid pictures of outdoor life in Venice—
notably the celebration of the Feast of Saint Mark
—in the palmy days of the Serene Republic, does
the "Master Mosaic-Workers" attract and hold our
interest. The author is no less successful in dealing
with the historical personages who figure in her
pages; in portraying the strange mixture of incorruptible honesty, jealous suspicion, and unsatisfied
ambition in the character of Bozza, and thereby
suggesting the undiscovered "explanation" of his
actions; in depicting the constant struggle in the
heart of old Sebastiano Zuccato between his affection
for his sons and his pride in their talent, and his
contempt for what was in his eyes a degrading profession; and if she has painted the Bianchini in
somewhat darker colors than history seems to warrant, we can easily make excuses for her, because
their treacherous machinations serve to bring out
in bolder relief the sentiment which appeals most
strongly to our emotions. The author tells us that
she promised the poor child who had read nothing
but "Paul and Virginia," that she would write a
story for him in which there should be no love, and
in which everything should end happily. She was
true to her promise, if the word "love" is taken
in its ordinary acceptation as applied to the art of

novel-writing; but it would be hard to conceive a truer, holier affection between man and woman than that which united the brothers Zuccato,— which led Valerio to share his brother's imprisonment, and Francesco to exclaim, when his brother's work was adjudged more meritorious than his own, "I drink to my master, Valerio Zuccato!"

PREFACE.

I WROTE the "Master Mosaic-Workers" in 1837 for my son, who had as yet read but one romance, "Paul and Virginia." That story was too trying for the nerves of a poor little child. He cried so much that I promised to write him a romance in which there should be no love, and where everything should turn out for the best. To add a little instruction to his pastime, I took a real fact in the history of art. The adventures of the mosaic-workers of St. Mark's are in the main true. I have woven in but a few embellishments, and have developed some characters which history only touches on.

I do not know why, but I have written few books with so much pleasure as this. It was in the country, during a summer as warm as the climate of Italy,

AUTHOR'S PREFACE.

which I had just left. I had never seen so many flowers and birds in my garden. Liszt was playing on the ground floor, and the nightingales, intoxicated with music and sun, sang themselves hoarse in the surrounding lilacs.

GEORGE SAND.

NOHANT, May, 1852.

TO MAURICE D.

YOU find fault with me, my child, for always telling you stories which end unhappily and make you sad, or with narratives so long, so long, that you fall sound asleep in the midst of them. Do you think, then, little one, that your old father can have cheerful thoughts after such a severe winter, after a spring so bleak, so cold, so productive of rheumatism? When the dreary north wind moans in our old fir trees, when the crane utters its mournful cry at the sound of the Angelus saluting the dim and chilly dawn, I can dream only of blood and misery. Great green spectres dance about my flickering lamp, and I arise uneasily to drive them from your bed. But the time is past when children believed in ghosts. You smile when we tell you of the superstition and terror which surrounded our childhood. Ghost stories which used to keep us wide awake and trembling in our beds until the dull break of day make you smile, and you sleep on. So you want a simple and natural story, hey, young man? I will try to recall one of those which the Abbé Panorio related at Beppa, when I was in Venice. The Abbé Panorio was of your opinion regarding stories. He was sated with the fantastic. The con-. fessions of old fanatical women had made him look upon witches and apparitions with horror. Neither was he much in favor of sentimentality. Love stories seemed to him very foolish; but, like you, he enjoyed the reveries of the lovers of nature, the labors and trials of artists. His stories were always founded on historic fact; and if they sometimes made us sad, they ended always with a consoling truth or a useful lesson.

It was during the beautiful summer nights, by the light of the soft full moon of the eastern sea, that, seated under an arbor all abloom, intoxicated with the perfume of grape and jasmine, we were enjoying our supper from midnight until two o'clock in the gardens of Santa-Margarita. Our companions were Assem Zuzuf, an honest merchant of Corcyra, Seigneur Lélio, the leading singer in the Fenice Theatre, Dr. Acrocéronius, the charming Beppa, and the excellent Abbé Panorio. A nightingale sang in its green cage suspended from the arbor which sheltered our table. At the sherbet, Beppa

DEDICATION.

tuned a lute, and sang with a voice even more melodious than that of the nightingale. The jealous bird often interrupted him with precipitate runs, wild outbursts of melody, or lyric declamation. Then we extinguished the candles, and the nightingale was silent. The moon tinted with delicate sapphires and bluish diamonds the crystals and silver flagons spread before us. Afar we heard the voluptuous swell of the sea, breaking against the flowery beach, and now and then the breeze wafted to us the sound of the slow, monotonous recitative of the gondoliers:—

"Intanto la bella Erminia fugge," etc.[1]

Then the abbé told us of the happy days of the Republic and its lordly customs, when his fatherland was at the zenith of its glory and power. At other times, also, he had taken pleasure in recalling its gayety and pomp. Although young, the abbé knew the history of Venice better than her oldest inhabitants. He had lovingly studied it in her monuments and public documents. He had also enjoyed searching her popular traditions for the details regarding the lives of some of her greatest artists. One day he told us a little anecdote relating to Tintoretto and

[1] "In the mean time, the beautiful Erminie runs (away)."

DEDICATION.

Titian, which I shall try to recall, if this warm breeze swaying our linden trees, and the lark continuing his ecstatic song among the clouds, are not interrupted by a gale, and if the breath of spring opening our lazy roses and expanding my heart deigns to blow over us until to-morrow morning.

THE MASTER MOSAIC-WORKERS.

I.

"BELIEVE me, Messer Jacopo, I am a most unhappy father. I shall never be consoled for this disgrace. We live in an age of decadency. Hereditary prestige no longer prevails. In my time every one tried to equal, if not to surpass, his parents. To-day, provided one makes a fortune, no one considers the means, no one fears to degrade the established standard. The nobleman turns shopkeeper; the master, workman; the architect, mason; the mason, hod-carrier. Where will it all end, holy Mother of God?"

Thus spoke Messire Sebastian Zuccato, a painter forgotten to-day, but noted in his time as the teacher of the illustrious master, Jacopo Robusti, better known to us by the name of Tintoretto.

"Ah! ah!" replied the master, who, through habitual preoccupation, was often extremely outspoken, "it is better to be a good workman than a commonplace master, a great mechanic than a poor artist, a—"

"Ah! ah! my dear master," exclaimed old Zuccato, a little piqued, "do you mean by poor artists, commonplace painters, the syndic of painters, the master of so many masters who are the glory of Venice, and form a grand constellation where you are set like a star among its dazzling rays, but where my pupil Titian shines with no less lustre?"

"Oh! oh! Master Sebastian," replied Tintoretto, calmly, "if such stars and such constellations shed their lustre on the Republic, if from your studio come forth so many great masters, beginning with the illustrious Titian, before whom I bow without jealousy or resentment, we do not live in an age of decadency, as you said just now."

"Ah, well! of course," said the dolorous old man, impatiently, "it is a good age, a fine age for the arts. But I cannot console myself with having contributed to its glory and being the last to enjoy it. What is it to me to have produced a Titian if no one remembers it, and no one cares? Who will know it a hundred years hence? Even to-day no one would know it but for the gratitude of this great man, who goes about everywhere singing my praises and calling me his dear compeer. But what does it all amount to? Ah! why did not Heaven allow me to be the father of Titian, that he might be called Zuccato, or I be called Vecelli? At least, my name would live from age to age, and a thousand years hence they would say, 'The head of that line was a good master.' But I have two sons false to my honor, faithless to the noble Muses,—two sons full of brilliant talent, who should have made my glory, who perhaps would have eclipsed Giorgione, Schiavone, the Bellini, Veronese, Titian, and even Tintoretto himself. Yes, I venture to say that, with their natural talents, and the advice which, in spite of my age, I still think I could give them, they might efface their ignominy, quit the ladder of the workman, and mount the scaffold of the painter. It is for you then, my dear master, to give me a new proof of the friendship with which you honor me, by joining Messer Tiziano in a last effort to curb the erring minds of these unfortunate boys. If you can reclaim Francesco, he will take it upon himself to bring back his brother; for Valerio is a young man without brains, I should say almost without capacity, if he were not my son, and if he had not occasionally given proof of intelligence by the fresco friezes he has drawn on the walls of his studio. My Checo is a very different man. He can handle the brush like a master, and knows how to impart to other artists those grand conceptions which they, and even you, as you have often told me, Messer Jacopo, do but execute. In addition to this, he is refined, energetic, persevering, restless, and ambitious. He has all the qualifications of a great artist. Alas! I shall never understand how he has allowed himself to follow such an evil course."

"I will do what you wish," replied Tintoretto; "but, first, I will tell you in all conscience what I think of your bitter opposition to the profession your sons have embraced. The mosaic art is not, as you call it, a low vocation; it is a true art, brought from Greece by able masters, of whom we should speak only with deep respect; for this art alone has preserved to us, still more than that of painting on metal, the lost traditions of Byzantine art. If it has transmitted them to us altered and hardly recognizable, it is none the less true that without it they would have been lost entirely. Canvas does not outlast the ravages of time. Apelles and Zeuxis have left only names. What gratitude should we not feel to-day towards those courageous artists, had they but immortalized their

THE MASTER MOSAIC-WORKERS.

works by the aid of crystal and marble! Moreover, the mosaic-work has preserved to us intact the traditions of color; and herein, so far from being inferior to painting, it has this advantage which cannot be denied: it resists the wear and tear of time, as well as the ravages of the atmosphere—"

"Since it resists so well," interrupted old Zuccato testily, "how comes it that the Seigniory is repairing all the domes of St. Mark's, which to-day are as bare as my skull?"

"Because, at the time when they were decorated with mosaics, Greek artists were scarce in Venice. They came from a distance, and remained but a short time. Their apprentices were hastily trained, and executed the works intrusted to them without knowing their business, and without being able to give to them the necessary solidity. Now that this art has been cultivated in Venice century after century, we have become as skilful as the Greeks ever were. The works of your son Francesco will be handed down to posterity, and he will be blessed for having placed upon the walls of our basilica imperishable frescos. The canvas upon which Titian or Veronese have flung their masterpieces will crumble to dust, and a day will come when our great masters will be known only by the mosaics of the Zuccati."

"Indeed, then," said the obstinate old man, "you might as well say that Scarpone, my shoemaker, is a greater master than the Almighty; for my foot, which is the work of the Divinity, will crumble to ashes, while my shoe will retain for ages the form and impress of my foot."

"But the color, Messer Sebastian, the color! Your comparison is worthless. What material manufactured by the hand of man could preserve the exact color of your flesh for an unlimited time, — while stone and metal, primitive and unchangeable substances, retain to the last grain of powder the Venetian color, the most beautiful in all the world, before which Buonarotti and all his Florentine school are forced to lower the flag? No, no, you are in the wrong, Master Sebastian, you are unjust, if you do not say, 'Honor to the engraver, the depositary and propagator of correct drawing! Honor to the mosaic-worker, the guardian and preserver of color!'"

"I am your humble servant," replied the old man. "Thanks for your good advice, Messer. It only remains for me to beseech you to see that my name is engraved upon my tomb with the title *Pictor*, so that it may be known, a year after, that there was in Venice a man of my name who handled the brush and not the trowel."

"Tell me, Messer Sebastian," replied the kindly master, interrupting him, "have you not seen the last works executed by your sons in the interior of the basilica?"

"God preserve me from ever seeing Francesco and Valerio Zuccato hoisted up by a rope like slaters, cutting enamel and handling mastic!"

"But you know, my dear Sebastian, that these works have obtained the greatest praise from the Senate, and the highest compensation from the Republic?"

"I know, Messer," answered Zuccato haughtily, "that there is on the ladders of the basilica of St. Mark a young man who is my oldest son, who for a hundred ducats a year abandons the noble profession of his fathers, in spite of the reproaches of his conscience and the humiliation of his pride. I know that there walks the streets of Venice a young man who is my second son, who, in order to pay for his idle pleasures and foolish extravagance, consents to sacrifice all his pride, hire himself out to his brother, throw aside the much too elegant apparel of the debauchee for the much too humble garb of the workman, set himself up for a nobleman in the gondolas in the evening, and play the part of a mason all day, and all to pay for the supper and serenade of the evening before. This I know, Messer, and I know nothing more."

"And I tell you, Master Sebastian," replied Tintoretto, "that you have two good and noble sons, two excellent artists, one of whom is industrious, patient, original, painstaking, in fact, an acknowledged master in his art; while the other, lovable, upright, genial, full of talent and enthusiasm, less steady at his work perhaps, but more ready with large ideas and lofty conceptions —"

"Yes, yes," retorted the old man, "ready with ideas, and with words even more so. Oh, yes, I know very well these theoretical people who *feel art*, as they say, who explain it, define it, exalt it, and do it no good. These are the lepers of the studio. They make the noise, others do the work. They come of too noble a race to work, or else they have so much talent they do not know what to do with it. Inspiration is the death of them. So, lest they should be too much inspired, they prattle and walk the streets from morning till night. Apparently it is for fear the emotion of art and manual labor will injure his health, that my son Valerio does nothing with his ten fingers, and lets his brains run away through his lips. This boy always makes me think of a piece of canvas on which some one has drawn, day after day, the first lines of a sketch without taking the pains to erase the preceding ones, presenting, after a little while, the odd spectacle of a multitude of incoherent lines, each one of which might have had an intention and an end, but not one of which would the artist, plunged in chaos, be able either to seize again or carry on."

"I admit that Valerio is a little dissipated and somewhat lazy," replied the master. "I shall take it upon myself to reproach him with this once more, taking advantage of the paternal right which he himself has given me by engaging himself voluntarily to my little Marie."

"And you permit this levity?" said the old painter, illy disguising the secret pleasure this circumstance caused him, confirmed by the mouth of Robusti himself. "You allow an artisan — not even an artisan, an apprentice — to dare to aspire, even in jest, to the hand of your daughter? Messer Jacopo, I tell you that, if I had a daughter, and if Valerio Zuccato instead of being my son were my nephew, I should not permit him to place himself in the ranks of her wooers."

"Oh, that concerns my wife," answered Robusti. "It will concern my daughter, when she shall be old enough to marry. Marie will have talent, considerable talent. I trust she will soon make portraits that I shall dare to sign, and which posterity will not hesitate to attribute to me. I hope she will make an illustrious name, and thereby win an honored position. The heritage of an independent fortune is assured to her through my work. So, whether she marries Valerio the apprentice, or Bartolommeo Bozza the apprentice of the apprentice, if it seems good to her, she will always be Marie Robusti, the daughter, pupil, and continuator of Tintoretto. There are girls who can marry to their liking, and not for their advantage. Young patrician girls care more for their pages than for the illustrious alliances offered them. Marie is patrician in her way. Let her act so. You know the child has a fancy for Valerio."

Old Zuccato shook his head, and did not answer, not wishing to manifest his joy and gratitude. However, the master perceived a great softening in his manner; and, after a sufficiently long discussion, in which Sebastian defended himself step by step, but with less asperity than in the beginning, he ended by letting himself be taken to the basilica of

St. Mark, where the brothers Zuccati were at that time completing the great mosaic of the dome over the inner door of the main entrance. The figures, taken from the visions of the Apocalypse, were executed after the very cartoons of Titian and Tintoretto.

II.

WHEN old Zuccato entered beneath this oriental cupola, where, on a foundation of shining gold, the colossal figures of the prophets and Apocalyptic phantoms loomed like terrible apparitions evoked in their dreams, he was seized, in spite of himself, with a superstitious fear, and, the emotion of the artist giving place for a moment to a religious feeling, he crossed himself, saluted the altar, the golden metal of which shone dimly at the farther end of the sanctuary, and, laying his cap on the pavement, recited inaudibly a short prayer.

When he had finished, he arose painfully from his knees, which were stiffened with age, and ventured to cast his eyes on the figures of the four Evangelists, which were the nearest to him. But, as his sight was dim, he could only take in the general effect, and, turning to Tintoretto, he said:—

"It cannot be denied that these great masses are impressive. Pure charlatanism, after all.— Ah! ah! Monsieur, is that you?"

These last words were addressed to a tall, pale young man, who, hearing the cupola re-echo the sharp, broken tones of his father's voice, had hastily come down from his scaffolding to meet him. Francesco, having struggled gently and perseveringly against his father's wishes, had ended by following his vocation, and abstaining from frequent interviews which could but rekindle this subject of discord. But he was on all occasions humble and respectful towards the author of his being. In order to give him a more suitable welcome, he had hastily washed his face and hands, thrown aside his apron, and donned his silk mantle embroidered with silver, which one of his young apprentices had given him. Thus attired, he was as handsome and elegant as the most fashionable of noblemen. But his thoughtful face and the gravity of his smile evinced the exalted conscientiousness and sacred self-respect of the artist.

Old Zuccato eyed him from head to foot, and, struggling with his feelings, said ironically: "Ah, well, Monsieur, how shall we manage in order to admire your masterpieces? If they were not glued to the wall body and soul, we might ask you to detach some of them. But you have better understood what is for the interest of your glory, by placing them all so high that no eye can reach them."

"Father," replied the young man, modestly, "the happiest day of my life would be that on which these feeble productions might obtain from you a look of indulgence. But your strong will is a much greater obstacle than the distance which separates you from this dome. If it were in my power to overcome your prejudice, I do not doubt that, with my brother's assistance, I could succeed in leading you to the top of these planks, where you could take in at one glance all the figures which are hidden from you at this moment."

"Your brother!" said the old growler. "And where is your brother? Will he not condescend to come down from his sky of glass-ware, to welcome me in his turn?"

"My brother has gone out," said Francesco; "otherwise he would have hastened, like me, to change his clothes and come to kiss your hand. I expect him every moment, and he will be very happy to find you here."

"Doubtless he will come gay and singing as usual, will he not, his cap on one side, his eye restless, his gait unsteady? A workman who absents himself at working hours to go to the tavern will be a very safe guide, I think, to help me in climbing your ladders."

"Father, Valerio is not at the tavern. He has gone for some material for our work. I sent him to the factory to get some patterns of enamel which had to be prepared expressly for me, the exact shade of which is very hard to obtain."

"In that case you will wish him good day for me. It is full two leagues from here to Murano, and the tides are contrary, which may be understood in two ways. This is why he will have drunk so much wine in the company of his oarsmen; and the oar will be no better implement in his hands to-day than the trowel."

"Father, some one has made false statements to you in regard to Valerio," replied the young man, earnestly. "He loves pleasure and Cyprus wine, I admit, but he is none the less diligent in consequence. He is an excellent workman, and when I charge him with a commission, he performs it with a precision and understanding that leave nothing to be desired."

"Valerio! here is Messer Valerio!" cried a voice from the top of the scaffoldings. It was the voice of Bartolommeo, the apprentice, who, through one of the lights in the cupola, had seen the disembarkation from the gondolas at the steps of the Piazzetta.

A few moments after, Valerio entered the basilica, followed by his workmen carrying a large basket of glass-ware. He was singing in a clear and resonant voice, with none too much respect for the holy place, the refrain of a love song. But as soon as he saw his father he lifted his cap and stopped singing. Then he approached him without embarrassment, and embraced him with the confidence and candor of an upright soul.

Zuccato was struck with his steadiness, and his bright and guileless manner.

Valerio was the handsomest fellow in Venice. He was not so tall, but better proportioned and more robust than his brother. His fine face expressed at a first glance only good nature, courage, and frankness. It required some attention to discover in his great blue eyes the sacred fire that slumbered there, often under a shade of quiet indifference, whose lustre, although not altered, was at least veiled, by a slight expression of fatigue.

This half-pallor ennobled his beauty and tempered the serene audacity of his look. He was exceedingly particular in his dress, and set the fashion for the most brilliant lords of the Republic. He was sought after by them and by the ladies on account of his talent for composing and designing ornaments, which were afterwards executed under his direction, in gold and silver embroidery on the richest materials. A velvet cap surrounded by a Grecian pattern after the style of Valerio Zuccato, the fringe of a dress made after his models, the border of a mantle of cloth of gold in shaded silk embroidery interwoven with chains or flowers or leaves after the manner of his Byzantine mosaics, were, in the eyes of a lady of rank or a polished nobleman, objects of the first necessity. Valerio made considerable money by this occupation, which diverted him after his labors and pleasures, and which he carried on in his little studio at Santi-Filippo-e-Giacomo, under the shadow of a certain mystery, into which, however, every one was benevolently initiated. His striking appearance, his amiability, his relations with the noble lords and the happy workmen that filled his studio at all hours, would necessarily have drawn him into a life of pleasure, had not his natural activity and his fidelity in filling all professional engagements preserved him from falling into excesses which would have ruined his genius.

A tender and unalterable friendship united the two brothers. They succeeded in conquering the feigned repugnance of old Zuccato, and, having erected two ladders, one on either side of that on which he ventured to ascend, they supported him, and took him to the very last staging of their scaffolding. Tintoretto, already old, but still sure-footed and accustomed to making his studio in the vast cupolas of the basilica, had followed them, in order to witness the surprise of Sebastian. The feeling of religious terror which the old man had experienced at first, gave place to an involuntary ecstasy when, having arrived on a level with the imposing figures of the Prophets and Evangelists, which occupied the first tier, he saw all the completed portions of this wonderful composition. Here was the Translation of the Virgin treated after Salviati; farther on, the Resurrection of Lazarus, a frightful scene, where the corpse, clothed in the pure tone of the winding sheet, seemed to float with uncertainty on the brilliant background of the wall. Titian's Saint Mark, a massive figure borne by the crescent moon as if in a boat, seemed raised to the resplendent heavens by an ascending movement perceptible to the eye; the great festoon of the arch, supported by beautiful winged angels, and, above all these numerous *chefs-d'œuvre*, the Vision of Saint John, where the damned are precipitated into hell, while the elect of the Lord, clothed in white and mounted on white horses, vanish in the subdued splendor and mysterious light of the cupola, like a flock of swans in the rosy mists of morning.

Zuccato tried again to wrestle with the admiration which he felt, by attributing the cause of his sudden emotion to the effect of the light playing upon the objects, to the favorable situation and the imposing size of the figures. But when Tintoretto prevailed upon him to approach the festoon, in order to appreciate its details, he was obliged to admit that he never would have believed the mosaic art capable of such perfection, and that the little angels flying among the garlands would rival in color and form the paintings of the greatest masters.

But, always stingy of his praise, and indignant at his own covert satisfaction, the old man pretended that the only merit of the work lay in its correctness, and in the great amount of patience bestowed upon it.

"All the honor," said he, "belongs to the masters who drew the models of these groups and designed the details of these decorations."

"Father," replied Francesco, with modest pride, "if you will be so kind as to allow me to show you the cartoons of the masters, perhaps you will give us credit, if not of having created, at least of having understood our models with some intelligence."

"I wish you would," said Tintoretto. "I wish my cartoons of the Apocalypse to be the proof of the talent for painting which distinguishes Francesco and Valerio Zuccato from all artists of their class."

Several models were exhibited, and Sebastian could convince himself of the intelligence with which the Zuccati worked as masters after masters, drawing the elegant and chaste designs of their subjects themselves, and creating their marvellous color after the simple suggestion of the painter. Valerio, after a little urging on the part of his brother, acknowledged himself to be the author of many little figures, and, in his turn divulging Francesco's secret, he showed his father two beautiful archangels flying towards each other. One, enveloped in green drapery, was his own work; the other, dressed in turquoise blue, was the work of Francesco, composed and carried out without the assistance of any painter.

Zuccato allowed himself to be led towards these figures, which were really as beautiful as any of those whose models had been furnished. Francesco had given to his young archangel the features of his brother Valerio, and reciprocally Valerio's archangel was the portrait of Francesco. They had employed combinations of the utmost delicacy in executing this cherished work, and had modestly placed it in an obscure corner, where the gaze of the vulgar could not reach it. Old Zuccato remained for a long time motionless and dumb before this winged pair, and, confounded at seeing the arrogant error of his whole life so gloriously refuted, he flew into a violent passion. He descended the ladder, snatched his cloak roughly from the hands of Valerio, without deigning to say a word of encouragement either to him or to his brother, and, scarcely noticing Tintoretto, with a firmer step than one would have expected of him he sprang over the threshold of the basilica. But he had not gone down the first step, when, yielding to the imperious longing of his soul, he turned, and, opening his arms to his two sons, who flung themselves into them, he pressed them for a long time to his heart, bathing with his tears their beautiful heads.

III.

"COME on! Long life to good luck! By the body of the devil, the work progresses. Bring me some mastic, you little black monkey! Maso! do you hear me? By the devil, brother Vincent, don't monopolize all the apprentices. Send down some of your daubed-up seraphim, so that I may not be delayed. Ah, by the blood of Bacchus! if I throw my mallet at the head of that porpoise of a Maso, I fear it will be a long while before the Republic sees such another ugly face!"

Thus shouted from the top of his scaffoldings a red-headed giant, who was directing the works in the Chapel of St. Isidore, that part of the basilica of St. Mark having been intrusted to Dominique Bianchini, called the Red, and his two brothers, emulators and rivals of the Zuccati brothers in the mosaic art.

"Hold your tongue, you big bawler! Have a little patience, carrot-top!" cried, from his side, the peevish Vincent Bianchini, the eldest of the three brothers. "Haven't you got your apprentices? Make them stir themselves, and let mine attend to their business. Haven't you John Viscentin, that pretty white cheese from the Alps? Where have you sent Reazo, your bully with a cold in his head, who sings so fine in the choir on Sundays? I'll wager that all your boys are running to the tavern at the present moment to get a bottle of wine under cover of your name. If that's so, they won't come back very soon."

"Vincent," replied Dominique, "it's well for you you are my brother and partner; for I could, with one stroke of my foot, smash your scaffolding, and send your illustrious person and all your fine apprentices to study mosaic on the pavement."

"If you had only thought of it," said the rough voice of Gian Antonio Bianchini, the youngest of the three brothers, who was shaking the foot of the ladder on which Dominique was working, "I could prove to you that the highest perches are not always the safest. Not that I care any more for Vincent's hide than I do for your own, but I do not like bragging, do you understand; and for some days past I notice that you have assumed, sometimes towards him and sometimes towards me, a tone that is not to be endured."

The sullen Dominique looked darkly at the young Antonio, and let himself be shaken for a few moments without saying a word. Then, as soon as Antonio recommenced grinding his cement under the portico, he came down, threw aside his apron and cap, rolled up his sleeves, and prepared to give him a sound thrashing.

The priest, Alberto Zio, who was also a distinguished mosaic-worker, and who, mounted on a ladder, was at that moment repairing one of the panels of the outer door, hurried down to separate the combatants; and Vincent Bianchini, rushing from the end of the chapel, mallet in hand, prepared to take part in the fray, more from a feeling of resentment against Dominique than through any interest in Antonio.

The priest, after trying in vain to bring them back to more Christian feelings, in order to quiet them resorted at last to an argument which seldom failed of its effect.

"If the Zuccati overhear you," said he, "they will exult in your quarrels, and imagine that, thanks to their amiability and good sense, they work better than you do."

"That's so," said Dominique the Red, putting on his apron again. "We'll settle this affair this evening at the tavern. For the present, we must not put weapons in the hands of our enemies."

The other two Bianchini acquiesced in this opinion; and while each of them filled his *raclette* with newly prepared cement, Father Alberto entered into conversation with them.

"You are wrong, my children," said he, "in looking upon the Zuccati as your enemies. They are your rivals, that is all. If they follow different methods from yours, they appreciate no less the merit of your work. Indeed, I have often heard their first apprentice, Bartolommeo Bozza, say that your cementation is of a superior quality to theirs, and that the Zuccati candidly acknowledge it."

"As to Bartolommeo Bozza," replied Vincent Bianchini, "I say nothing against him: he is a good workman and a stanch fellow. I am on the point of making it worth his while to engage himself in my service. But do not talk to me of those Zuccati. There are no worse intriguers in the world, and if their talent were equal to their ambition they would surpass all their rivals. Fortunately idleness consumes them. The elder wastes his time imagining subjects that cannot be executed, and the younger carries on a contraband work at San Filippo, and eats the fruit of it with people above his station."

"The star of the Zuccati could be made to fall from the clouds in spite of the patronage of the painters," said the envious Dominique, "if any one cared to take the trouble."

"How so?" exclaimed the other two. "If you know a way to humiliate them, tell it, and your insults to us shall be forgiven."

"I care no more for you than for them," said Dominique. "Only I say that it is not impossible to prove that they do not earn their salary, for they are doing bad work, and are consequently stealing the public funds."

"For shame, Messer Dominique!" said the priest sternly. "Do not speak so of two men who enjoy the public esteem. You will lead people to think that you are jealous of their advantages."

"Yes, I am jealous of them," cried Dominique, stamping his foot. "And why shouldn't I be jealous? Isn't it an injustice on the part of the procurators to give them a hundred golden ducats a year while we have only thirty,—we, who have worked for nearly ten years on the genealogical tree of the Virgin? I venture to say that the Zuccati could not have accomplished half this enormous work, even if they had devoted all their lives to it. How many months does it take them to make the breadth of a dress, or a child's hand? Just watch them for a while, and you will see what their fine talent costs the Republic."

"They get on less quickly than you, it is true," replied the priest. "But what perfection in the design, what richness in the color!"

"If you were not a priest," replied Vincent, shrugging his shoulders, "one would know how to talk to you. You'd better go back to your confessional and your censer than be judging of things of which you know nothing."

"Messer, how dare you say that?" said Alberto, slightly offended. "You forget that I understood the business before you had the first notion of it, and that I am the best disciple under our common master, the ingenious Rizzo, the worthy successor of our gypsoplast masters."

"Ingenious as much as you choose, it does not require much imagination to work in mosaic. It requires what you lack, — you and your other priests and those lazy Zuccati, — strong arms, loins of iron, precision, and activity. Go say Mass, Father Alberto, and let us alone."

"Hush! no noise!" said Antonio. "There's that sullen old Zuccato going by. See how his sons escort him back, waving their caps and kissing their hands! Wouldn't you say it was a Doge attended by his senators? That one considers himself the most illustrious of men, and he does not know enough to let the cup alone."

"Silence!" said Vincent. "Here comes Messer Robusti to look at our work."

All three of them uncovered, more out of fear of his reputation as an artist than through any respect for his genius, which they were not capable of appreciating. Father Alberto went to meet him, and led him into the Chapel of St. Isidore. Tintoretto glanced at the incrusted panels, praised the repairs of the ancient Greek mosaics confided to the priest, and withdrew, bowing profoundly to the Bianchini without speaking to them. for he liked neither them nor their works.

IV.

THE day's work being ended, and the Zuccati having supped with their principal apprentices, Bozza, Marini, and Ceccato, (who later on became excellent artists,) in a little *bottega*,[1] where they were in the habit of meeting, under the *Procuraties*,[2] Valerio was preparing to hasten to his business or his pleasures, when his brother detained him, saying: —

"For to-day, my dear Valerio, you must sacrifice a part of your evening to me. I retire early, as you know. You will still have plenty of time after we have talked."

"I am willing," said Valerio, "but it is on condition that we take a skiff and have a little row; for I feel exhausted after the day's work, and cannot rest from one fatigue except by plunging into another."

[1] Shop or lunch-room.
[2] The palace of the Procurators, still in existence, near the Doge's palace.

"I do not know how to assist you in rowing," replied Francesco: "I have not your robust health, my dear Valerio, and, as I do not wish to miss my work to-morrow, I must not fatigue myself this evening; but, seeing that if I refuse you this diversion, I cannot prevail upon you to grant me two or three hours, I will go and ask Bozza to be of the party. He is a good fellow, and will not be in the way in the conversation I wish to have with you."

Bartolommeo Bozza readily accepted this invitation, and, hauling off one of the prettiest boats, he seized one oar, while Valerio took the other. Then, standing each at either extremity of the little skiff, they started it on its course with a vigorous stroke, and made it bound over the foaming waves. It was the hour when the fashionable world sought enjoyment on the Grand Canal in the cool air of the evening. The narrow little boat glided swiftly and stealthily among the gondolas, like a sea bird which flees from the pursuer, darting like an arrow through the green grasses. But in spite of the agility and the silence of the oarsmen, all eyes were fixed upon them, and all the ladies leaned forward on their cushions that they might gaze the longer upon the handsome Valerio, whose grace and strength excited the envy of the noblemen as well as of the gondoliers, and whose countenance showed a strange mingling of courage and artlessness.

Bozza was also strong and well formed, but thin and pale. A dull fire shone in his black eyes, a thick beard covered half his face, and although his features lacked regularity they attracted attention by their sad and haughty expression.

Thin and pale also, but noble and not proud, melancholy and not gloomy, Francesco Zuccato, reclining on a black velvet carpet in the bottom of the boat, supporting himself carelessly on his elbow, wrapped in a reverie which did not allow him to give much thought to the throng, shared with Valerio the admiration of the ladies, but did not perceive it.

When these three young men had gone up the length of the canal, they floated gently into the lagoon far from frequented places; then, allowing themselves to drift, they lay down in the bottom of the boat, under a beautiful sky studded with innumerable stars, and talked without constraint.

"My dear Valerio," said the elder of the Zuccati, "I am going to annoy you again with my admonitions; but it is absolutely necessary for you to lead a wiser life."

"You never could annoy me, my dearest brother,"

replied Valerio, "and your anxiety will always find me grateful. But I cannot promise you to alter my ways, I am so contented in this life I lead. I am as happy as a man can be. Why do you wish me to deprive myself of happiness, you who love me so much?"

"This life will kill you," answered Francesco. "It is impossible to follow, in the way that you do, a routine of pleasure and fatigue, dissipation and work."

"On the contrary, this life invigorates me and keeps me up," replied Valerio. "What is life in the designs of God, if not a continual alternation of pleasure and self-denial, lassitude and activity? Let me go on, and do not judge my strength by your own. Nature has certainly been inconsistent in not giving to the better and more estimable of us two the stronger constitution and the livelier disposition. But so many other gifts have fallen to you, my dear Francesco, that you cannot very well envy me these."

"I do not envy you them," said Francesco, "although they are the most precious of all, and are in themselves enough to make one happy. It is sweet to me to think that a brother, whom I love more than myself, does not suffer in his body and soul the ills and weariness that prey upon me. But this is not the sole question. You certainly owe your position to the friendship of illustrious masters, to the protection of the Senate, and to the kindness of the Procurators."

"I, my brother?" cried the indifferent young man. "Save the friendship of our dear comrade Titian and the kindness of Robusti,— two men whom I venerate, — save the affection of my father and that of my brother, which I prefer to everything in the world, all the rest is in my eyes of little account. Two bottles of Cyprus would console me any time for the loss of my employment and the disgrace of the Senate."

"At least you value honor," said Francesco gravely, "the honor of your father's name, of your own, for which I am responsible, and to which my own is pledged."

"Certainly," said Valerio, quickly raising himself on his elbow. "What are you driving at?"

"To tell you that the Bianchini are plotting against us, and that they can make us lose, not only the advantageous position and fine salary to which you have the wisdom to prefer the wine of Cyprus and pleasure parties, but also the confidence of the Senate, and consequently the respect of the citizens."

"By Bacchus!" said Valerio, "I should like to see them do it. Let us go and find these Bianchini, if that is the case, and challenge them. They are three; our friend Bozza will be our third. The right is on our side. We will make a vow to the Madonna, and be delivered from these traitors."

"That would be all foolishness," said Francesco. "The Divine Power has not declared itself in favor of those who give provocation, and we should be doing so if we were to call to combat men against whom we have no proven grievance. Moreover, the Bianchini would respond to the offer to cross swords by sharpening their stilettos in order to stab us in the dark, as it is their custom to do. They are insatiable foes. They will never provoke us openly while we are under the protection of those in power, and when they let us know they hate us, it is all up with us. Indeed, this is what I am a little afraid of. Vincent, always so polite to me, no longer bows to me when I pass before his scaffolding. This morning, as we were escorting our father back to the foot of the steps of the basilica, I thought I saw under the portico the three Bianchini watching us maliciously and ridiculing us. The hatred, for a long time pent up in the bottom of their souls, begins to show in their eyes. Bozza can tell you, moreover, that many a time after the close of day, or in the morning when he has been the first to come to work, he has surprised Vincent or Dominique Bianchini on our scaffoldings, studying with the closest attention the least details of our work."

"Bah! all that proves nothing. If they do not recognize us, it is because they are naturally rude. If they looked askance at us this morning, it was because they envied us the happiness of having a good father. If they examine our work, it is because they wish to ascertain the cause of our superiority. Should these motives cause anxiety?"

"Why, then, instead of talking naturally with Bozza when he meets them on the scaffolding, do they hastily withdraw by the opposite ladders like guilty people?"

"If I meet them myself," cried Valerio, clinching his fist, "they will have to explain themselves, or, by Bacchus! I'll make them come down faster than they went up."

"That would only increase the evil; for to revenge the one whom you will have insulted the other two will league themselves against you until death. Believe me, 'Honesty is the best policy.' Let us be calm, and sustain the noble attitude that becomes us as gentlemen. A generous-hearted line of conduct may perhaps bring them round, or at least it will prove them guilty in their animosity, and, if they persecute us, we shall obtain redress."

"But indeed, brother, how can they persecute us? What power have they to injure us? Can they prove that we do not work as well as they do?"

"They will say that we do not work as rapidly, and it will be easy for them to prove it."

"And we can prove that it is easy to work quickly when one works badly, and that perfection will not allow of haste."

"That is not very easy to prove. Between ourselves be it said, the *Procurator-Cassiere* commissioned to examine the work is not an artist. He sees in mosaic work only an application of colored particles more or less brilliant. Perfection of tone, beauty of design, ingenuity of composition, are nothing to him. He sees what strikes the fancy of the common people, the brilliancy and rapidity of the work. Did I not try in vain the other day to make him understand that the old pieces of gilded crystal used by our ancestors, and a little tarnished by time, were more favorable to color than those manufactured to-day? 'Indeed, you make a mistake,

Messer Francesco,' said he, ' in handing over to the Bianchini all the gold of modern manufacture. The commissioners have decided that the old will do mixed with the new. I cannot see why you keep the earlier ones for yourself. Do you think that the mixture of the old with the new would have a bad effect? If so, you seem to consider yourself a better judge than the Procurators of the Commission.'"

"And I could hardly help laughing at you," interrupted Valerio, "when you answered him so seriously, ' My lord, I have no such insolent pretensions.'"

"But did I not try in vain to make him understand that this brilliant gold hurt the faces, and completely ruined the effect of color? that my drapery could not be made effective except on gold a little red in tone? and that if I had made use of shining backgrounds, I should have been obliged to sacrifice all the shading, and to make the flesh violet without modelling, and draperies without folds and without lights?"

"And he gave you an unanswerable reply and in a very dry tone," said Valerio, laughing. "'The Bianchini do not scruple to do it,' said he, 'and their mosaics please the eye much better than yours.' What need of worrying yourself after such a decision as that? Suppress the shadows, cut a breadth of material from a great plate of enamel and lay it over the breast of Saint Nicaise, render Saint Cecilia's beautiful hair with a badly cut tile, a pretty lamb for Saint John the Baptist with a handful of quicklime, and the commission will double your salary, and the public clap its hands. Really, my brother, you who dream of glory, I do not understand how you can pledge yourself to the worship of art."

"I dream of glory, it is true," replied Francesco, "but of a glory that is lasting, and not the vain popularity of a day. I should like to leave an honored name, if not an illustrious one, and make those who examine the cupolas of St. Mark's five hundred years hence say, 'This was the work of a conscientious artist.'"

"And who tells you that five hundred years hence the public will be more enlightened than it is to-day?" said Bozza, in a rough voice, breaking the silence for the first time.

"At least there will be connoisseurs to revise the judgment of the public, and it is the connoisseurs of all time that it is my ambition to please. Is it a blameworthy ambition, Valerio?"

"It is a noble ambition, but it is an ambition, and

THE MASTER MOSAIC-WORKERS.

all ambition is a malady of the soul," answered the young Zuccato.

"A malady," replied Francesco, "without which intelligence would have nothing to feed on, and would languish in the dark without enlightening the world. It is the wind which draws the spark from the charcoal, which fans the flame and spreads it afar. Without this celestial breeze there would be no warmth, no light, no life."

"I do not consider myself dead," said Valerio. "Nevertheless, this tempestuous breeze has never blown over me. I feel that the spark of life radiates at all times through my heart and my brain. Provided I am warmed by the divine flame and feel myself alive, it matters little whether the light emanates from myself or from something else. All light comes from the divine fire. What is the aureole of the human head? Glory to uncreated genius! The glory of man is no more in himself than the sun is in the water which reflects its image."

"Perhaps," said Francesco, raising to heaven his great brown eyes wet with tears, "perhaps it is foolishness and vanity to believe one's self anything because, possessing the power to approach the ideal in thought, he apprehends the beautiful a little better than other men. However, in what should a man glory, if not in that?"

"Why is it necessary for a man to glory in anything? Provided he enjoys himself, is he not happy enough?"

"Is not glory the most sensible, the most violent, the most intense of all joys?" said Bozza, in an incisive tone, turning his eyes toward Venice.

It was the hour when the Queen of the Adriatic, like a beauty bedecking herself with diamonds for a ball, began to light her lamps, and the still waters, accustomed to basking in her splendor, in mute admiration reflected her fiery garlands.

"You distort words, friend Bartolommeo," said the young Valerio, giving a strong pull on the oar in the phosphorescent water, causing a pale light to play about the black sides of the boat. "The most intense of human joys is love; the most sensible is friendship; the most violent is indeed glory. But when you say violent, you say keen, terrible, and dangerous."

"But cannot one say that this violent joy is the most elevated of all?" replied Francesco, gently.

"I could not think so," answered Valerio. "The sweetest, noblest, most beneficent thing in life is love. It is to feel and conceive the beau ideal.

Therefore we must love all that approaches it, dream of it without ceasing, seek it everywhere, and grasp it as we find it."

"That is to say," returned Francesco, "to hug vain phantoms, seize dim reflections, make solid flickering shadows, worship the spectre of one's own fancies. Is that to enjoy and to possess?"

"Brother, if you were not somewhat ill," said Valerio, " you would not talk like this. The man who wishes in this life anything better than this life affords, is a proud man who blasphemes, or an ungrateful man who suffers. There are enough elevated pleasures for any one who knows how to love. Were there nothing but friendship on the earth, man would have no right to complain. If I had only you in the world, I should still bless Heaven. I have never imagined anything better, and if God had permitted me to create a brother I should not have been able to create anything so perfect as Francesco. Go to! God alone is a great artist, and what we in our days of foolishness ask of Him is not worth what He in his immutable wisdom gives us."

"Ah! my dear Valerio," said Francesco, folding his brother in his arms, "you are right. I am proud and ungrateful. You are worth more than both of us, and you are indeed a living proof of what you say. Yes, indeed, my soul is sick. Heal me with your tenderness, you whose soul is so healthy and so strong. Holy Virgin, pray for me! for I have been very guilty, having so good a brother, in allowing myself to give way to the sin of despondency."

"Nevertheless," replied Valerio, smiling, "the proverb says, 'There is no great artist without much sadness.'"

"And without a little hatred," added Bozza, with a gloomy air.

"Oh, proverbs are always half a lie," said Valerio, "for the reason that all proverbs, having their counterpart, express falsehood and truth at the same time. Francesco is a great artist, and I would pledge my body and soul that he never knew hatred."

"Never toward others," said Francesco; "toward myself very often, and herein lies the guilt of my pride. I always want to be better and more skilful than I am. I would like to be loved for my merit, not on account of my suffering."

"You are loved for both one and the other," replied Valerio. "But perhaps all men are not fitted to content themselves with affection. Perhaps without the need of being admired there would be no great artists, no masterpieces. The praise of the uneducated is a commendation one does not care for, but we find it indispensable. This need is so inexplicable that it must serve some purpose in the designs of God."

"It serves to make us suffer, and God is sovereignly unjust," said Bozza, lying down again in the bottom of the boat in an attitude of despair.

"Do not speak so," said Valerio. "See, my poor boy, how beautiful the sea is down there, below the horizon! Hear how that passing guitar sighs with sweet harmonies! Have you not a sweetheart, Bozza? Are we not your friends?"

"You are artists," answered Bozza, "and I am only an apprentice."

"That does not prevent us from loving you."

"It should not prevent you from loving me; but it prevents me from loving you as much as I should if I were your equal."

"Indeed! in that case I should not love the nobility," said Valerio, "for I am an artist only in name; I am, to tell the truth, only an artisan. All those whom I love are above me, beginning with my brother, who is my master. My father was a good painter; Vicelli and Robusti are giants before whom I am nothing. Nevertheless, I love them, and

I never dream of suffering on account of my inferiority. Artists! artists! you are all children of the same mother. She calls herself *Covetousness*, and you are all indebted to her more or less. That is what consoles me for being a simpleton."

"Do not say that, Valerio," replied his elder brother. "If you cared to take the pains, you would be the first mosaic-worker of your time. Your name would efface that of Rizzo, and mine would come only after yours."

"I should be very sorry for that. By Saint Theodore! May you be always the first! Holy Idleness! save me from such an unfortunate honor!"

"Do not utter such blasphemy, Valerio; art is above all affection."

"Whoever loves art loves glory," added Bozza, always sad and doleful, like the blast of a big brass trumpet breaking in on a sweet and joyous song. "Whoever loves glory is willing to sacrifice everything to it."

"Many thanks," said Valerio; "as for me, I shall never sacrifice anything to it. And yet I love art, you know it, both of you, although they accuse me of loving only wine and women; and indeed I must love it well, since I devote half a life to it, which I feel tempted to give entirely to pleasure.

Never am I so happy as when I am at work. When I succeed, I feel like tossing my cap away up above the great tower of St. Mark's. If I fail, nothing disheartens me, and the kind of anger I experience against myself is still a pleasure such as one realizes on a restive horse, a swelling sea, or in stimulating wine. But the approbation of others does not incite me any more than does a tip of the hat from my lords, the Bianchini. When Francesco, my other self, says to me, 'That is well done,' I am satisfied. When my father, looking at my archangel, smiled in spite of himself this morning, although he knit his brows, I was happy. Supposing the *Procurator-Cassiere* should say that Dominique the Red does better than I, so much the worse for the *Procurator-Cassiere*; I shall not cry. Let the good people of Venice find that I have not enough brick-dust in my flesh, nor enough ochre in my draperies, *Evviva giumento!*[1] If you were not so foolish, you would not make me laugh so much, and that would be too bad, for I laugh with all my heart."

"Happy, thrice happy carelessness!" said Francesco.

Talking thus they came back to the city. When they were near the shore, "Before I leave you," said Valerio, "we must come to an understanding.

[1] Long life to the donkey!

Of what do you complain? What do you ask of me? That I give up pleasure? You might as well try to hinder water from running down hill."

"That you should take your pleasures less publicly," answered Francesco, "and that you give up, for a time at least, your studio at San Filippo. All that might be wrongly interpreted. People are wondering already how the great number of arabesques which you design, and the lesser occupations to which you lend yourself, can be reconciled with what you do at the basilica. If I did not know your untiring activity, I should not understand it myself; and if with my own eyes I did not see your work progress, I should be inclined to think that two or three hours' sleep after nights of pleasure and excitement would hardly suffice for a man devoted all day to hard work. Do not let your numerous acquaintances, especially these talkative noblemen, come to visit you so continually at the basilica. Such an honor hurts the pride of the Bianchini. They say that these young people make you lose your time, — that they distract you from your work to occupy yourself with trifles. For instance, this pleasure society which you have started, and which has caused so much talk among all the tradesmen of the city."

"Alas!" cried Valerio, "it is just on this account that I am in such haste to leave you this evening. They expect me to regulate the costumes. There is no such thing as withdrawing, and you, Francesco, are pledged to take part."

"I am pledged to it provided the affair does not begin until after St. Mark's, because by that time I hope to have my cupola finished."

"I said so both on your account and mine; but you can readily see that two or three hundred young men eager for pleasure will not easily understand the arguments of one who, unlike them, cares solely for work. They have declared that, if I refuse to be with them immediately, the company will fall through, — that nothing is possible without me. Therefore they have already reproached me severely, alleging that I had started them, that the expenses have been contracted, the refreshments ordered, and that so long a delay would give a victory to the other companies. In short, they have done so much that I stand pledged, both for you and myself, to hoist the banner of the Companions of the Lizard in fifteen days. We will open with a grand game of rings and a splendid banquet, to which each member will be expected to bring a young and beautiful lady."

THE MASTER MOSAIC-WORKERS.

"Do you not think this foolishness will put back your work?"

"Long life to pleasure! but I defy it to hinder me from working when the hour for work strikes. There is time for all, brother. So I can count on you?"

"You may enter my name, and through your hands I will deposit my fee; but I shall not appear at the fête. I do not wish it said that the two Zuccati were off duty at the same time. It must be understood that, when one is enjoying himself, the other works for two."

"Dear brother," cried Valerio, clasping him in his arms, "I will work for four the day previous, and you will be at the fête. Come, it will be a splendid affair, and for a noble purpose,—a festival thoroughly democratic and thoroughly fraternal. It shall not be said that noblemen alone have the right to enjoy themselves, and that the working men have religious confraternities only. No, no! the artist is not set apart to do penance always! The rich fancy that we are made to expiate their sins. Come, Bartolommeo, you will be there also; I am going to enter your name; it will put you to a little expense. If you have no money, I have, and I will be responsible for everything. *Au revoir*, dear friends, till to-morrow. Dearest brother, you will not say that I have not listened to your advice with the respect due to an elder brother. Come, tell me that you are satisfied with me."

So saying, Valerio sprang lightly on the shore of the ducal palace, and disappeared under the flitting shadows of the colonnade.

V.

THAT same evening, towards midnight, Bozza, returning from the house of his sweetheart, more sad and careworn than usual, weary of love, weary of work, and weary of life, was walking with great strides on the solitary shore. A blustering wind had arisen, the waves were beating against the marble quays, and mysterious voices seemed to mutter words of hatred and malediction under the black arcades of the old palace.

Suddenly he found himself face to face with a man whose heavy and echoing tread had not been able to rouse him from his reverie. By the light of a lantern fastened to a floating pier Bozza and the other nocturnal promenader met, and, stopping abruptly, eyed each other from head to foot. Bartolommeo, thinking this man might have some evil design, placed his hand upon his stiletto; but, contrary to his expectation, Vincent Bianchini, for it was he, touched his cap, and saluted him courteously.

Vincent, like his brother Dominique, was a coarse fellow and a wicked man. Less brutal in appearance, and capable in spite of his lack of education of assuming tolerably good manners, exceedingly cunning, skilled in lying, the result of his struggles to free himself from the damaging accusations brought against him by the Council of Ten, he was certainly the most dangerous of the three Bianchini.

"Messer Bartolommeo," said he, "I have just come from a place where I thought I should see you, and where I am very glad you had not, like me, the curiosity to creep in on the sly."

"I do not know what you mean, Messer Vincenzo," replied Bozza, bowing and trying to pass him.

Vincent accommodated his step to that of Bozza, without seeming to notice his desire to avoid him.

"You probably know," said he, "that the principal members of the new company have just held a meeting to talk over the statutes and the rules for admission.

"Possibly," said Bozza. "It matters very little to me, Messer Bianchini. I am not a man of pleasure."

"But you are a man of honor, and that is why it gave me pleasure not to see you among the auditors of this fine assembly."

THE MASTER MOSAIC-WORKERS.

"What do you mean?" exclaimed Bozza, stopping short.

"I mean to say, my dear Bartolommeo," replied Vincent, "that if you had been there things would have gone very differently, and perhaps there would have been a little noise. Besides, it would be better for everything to be arranged, for an affair so childish does not deserve—"

"Come, speak out, Messer, I beg you," said Bozza, impatiently. "Has anything occurred which touches my honor?"

"Oh, no, not personally perhaps, but along with others you have received an insult. This is what happened. You know that the new company is to be formed, like the other pleasure societies, of members chosen from different professions, emulators of each other in riches and talent. This company had agreed to receive all those who belonged to the corporation of glass-workers who were rich enough and cared enough for pleasure to wish to be admitted. Architects, glaziers, metal-workers, in fact, all the avocations which are represented by the work in the basilica, were to furnish their candidates. That settled, it simply remained to register the names of these candidates; and the founders of the company, having at their head Messer Valerio

THE MASTER MOSAIC-WORKERS.

Zuccato, your master, forthwith met for this purpose. But would you believe that this artist, so noted for his amiability and popularity, would have shown himself full of pride and contempt in regard to the greater part of the proposed admissions? Yes, indeed, he took upon himself to act the part of a gentleman, of a Senator in fact. He declared that whoever was not a master in some profession or other was not fit to enjoy himself in his company. Many opposed him, and some went so far as to say that certain apprentices were more economical and more talented than their masters, and consequently had more money and more influence. This is what he never would listen to, and he expressed himself in terms so haughty and severe that he offended everybody. At this moment I happened to be near him without his seeing me, and some one said to him, 'If you push the matter so far, will you not feel sorry for Bozza, that honest fellow who works so well, and is so fond of you and your brother?' 'If my apprentice is admitted into the company,' said Valerio, 'I shall withdraw.' In spite of that, the opinion of the majority ruled, and members will be admitted, provided always that the company judges them worthy to rank next to the mastership in their respective vocations."

Bozza did not reply to this speech; but Vincent Bianchini, who observed him closely, saw, by his nervous step and a jerking movement of his arms under his cloak, that he was very much annoyed.

However, Bartolommeo controlled himself, for he did not put absolute faith in the words of Bianchini. The latter, seeing that he must not allow the wound to heal, added in a careless tone, "It is a pity, after all, that a fellow so refined and so amiable should allow himself to be puffed up with vanity. Intercourse with the aristocracy must have been the cause of this unfortunate turn of affairs. It does an artist no good to mingle with people above his class."

"There is no class above the artist," replied the young apprentice, angrily. "If Valerio thinks more of anything else than of his art, he is not worthy of the title he bears."

"This foolish vanity," continued Bianchini, calmly, "is a family failing. Sebastian Zuccato despises his children because he is a painter and they are mosaic-workers. Francesco, his oldest son, who ranks among the first in his art, despises his brother because he seems a step below him, and he in turn despises his apprentice—"

"Do not say he despises me, Messer," said Bozza

in a hollow voice. "He dares not. Do not say that any one despises me, for, by the blood of Christ! I will teach you the contrary."

"If you are despised by a fool," answered Bianchini, with hypocritical calmness, "this contempt will turn to your glory. There are people whose esteem is an insult."

"Such is not the case between Valerio and myself," said Bozza, trying to control the passions which were rankling in his heart.

"I hope not," replied Vincent. "Nevertheless, I cannot conceive what he could have said of you to the person who pronounced your name, for he whispered to him, and I knew of whom he was speaking only by the manner in which he drew his cap down over his eyes, and pulled his coat collar up to his ears, in order to mimic and ridicule you. At the same time he frowned and imitated your gesture, causing the confidant of his foolish pleasantry to burst out laughing."

"And who was it that dared to laugh?" cried Bozza, drawing his cap down over his eyes, in spite of himself, clinching his fist and striking his breast, — the very gesture which, according to Bianchini, Valerio had turned into ridicule.

"Indeed, I cannot tell you," answered Bianchini.

"I could not see his face, because as usual Valerio had drawn about him a lot of listeners who were devouring his witticisms. When I succeeded in getting through the crowd, Valerio had changed his interlocutor, and was speaking of other things; but they were laughing still in the place he had just left.

"Very well!" exclaimed the wretched young man, "I thank you for telling me this: perhaps I shall find an opportunity to reward you for it."

Saying this, Bozza quickened his step, and Bianchini watched him for some time, his black plume tossing in the blustering wind. Then he lost sight of him, and, congratulating himself for having pierced the shield at the first blow, he remained for a long while motionless on the foamy bank, absorbed in his spiteful thoughts and wicked designs.

VI.

THE sun had scarcely begun to gild the tips of the white cupolas of St. Mark's, and the gondoliers of the Grand Canal still lay sleeping on the bank at the foot of the Leonine Column, when the basilica began to fill with workmen. The apprentices, arriving first, erected the ladders, assorted the enamel, and ground the cement, singing all the while and whistling and talking in a loud voice in spite of the distress of good Father Alberto, who tried in vain to remind these young scatterbrains of the solemnity of the place and the presence of the Lord.

If the exhortations of the priest mosaic-worker did not have much effect under the majestic cupola where the school of the Zuccati was at work, he could at least give vent to his zeal and ease his conscience by long and severe reprimands. He was never interrupted by a rude word nor an insulting laugh; for if these pupils had their master Valerio's gayety, ardor, and vivacity, they had also his gentleness, his goodness, and his pious respect for age and virtue.

But things went very differently in the Chapel of St. Isidore, where the Bianchini family, surrounded by wild and undisciplined apprentices, could not maintain order save by savage yells and terrible threats. When a lewd song reached the ears of Alberto, he could do nothing but cross himself, and his grief found expression in stifled exclamations and heavy sighs; but when, above all the coarse wrangling and brutal invectives which this set of workmen indulged in, the terrible voice of Dominique the Red came thundering under the echoing arches of the basilica, the poor priest was obliged to stop an ear with one hand, and with the other to hold on to one of the rungs of his ladder to prevent his falling.

During these days the master mosaic-workers arrived early, and set to work almost as soon as their apprentices. The Feast of Saint Mark was drawing near. On this solemn day was to take place the dedication of the basilica, entirely restored, and decorated with new paintings by the greatest masters of the age. After ten, fifteen, and twenty years of assiduous labor, they were to be judged publicly, regardless, it was said, of the patronage of the one class or the hatred of the other. It was to be a great day for all the workmen, from the first of the illustrious painters to the least of the daubers,— from the architect with his sublime conceptions to the docile workman who cut the stone and mixed the mortar. Rivalry, jealousy, buoyant expectation or sinister fear,—all the good and bad passions which the thirst for glory and the greed for gain awaken in men, whatever their position in art or business, were aroused unceasingly under these domes resounding with a thousand noises. Here was heard abusive language, there the joyous song, and further on the jest; above, the hammer; below, the trowel; now the dull and continuous thud of the *tampon* on the mosaics, and anon the clear and crystal-like clicking of the glass ware rolling from the baskets on to the pavement in waves of rubies and emeralds; then the fearful grating of the scraper on the cornice, and finally the sharp rasping cry of the saw in the marble, to say nothing of the low Masses said at the end of the chapel in spite of the racket. With all this was mingled the sound of the impassive ticking of the clock, the heavy vibrations of the bells, and the cries of a thousand domestic animals, imitated with rare perfection by the little apprentices in order to make Father Alberto, always duped by this trick, turn his head quickly and drop his work, which he never resumed until he had made the sign of the cross in expiation of what he was pleased to call his giddiness.

If the pupils of the Zuccati were more refined and innocent in their sport than those of the Bianchini, they were not much less noisy. Francesco rarely imposed silence upon them. Absorbed in his work, the patient and melancholy artist was wholly oblivious to all the confusion of his boisterous studio; moreover, provided the work suited him, he did not object to a gayety which pleased Valerio and enhanced his zeal. Valerio was really the idol of his apprentices. If he spurred them on without relaxation, and often enjoyed a good-natured criticism at their expense, at heart he loved them as his children, and charmed away their fatigue by his perpetual cheerfulness. Every day he had new and extravagant stories to tell them, every day he sang a song more ridiculous than that of the day before. If he saw a foolish fellow make a blunder, and deny it through pride, or persist in it through ignorance, he set all the school laughing at him, and daubed his face with his brush. But if a good pupil sincerely acknowledged his fault, or blushed in silence at an involuntary mistake, he went to him, took his tools, and in a few minutes repaired the error, and encouraged him either by gentle words or by saying nothing, in order not to draw upon the mortified apprentice the attention of his comrades. So it is true to say, that, if Francesco was loved and respected, Valerio was adored in his school, and his pupils would have thrown themselves from the top of the grand cupola to the pavement of the Place St. Mark to please him.

Bartolommeo Bozza alone, always cold and reticent, took no part in this merriment and enthusiasm. Francesco was much impressed with his work, uniformly correct and solid, and with the austerity of his manners. His sadness seemed to him to call for sympathy, and he liked to say that this dark and mysterious youth would, in the future, become a great artist. As to Valerio, although he found little pleasure in the company of Bartolommeo, he was too kind-hearted not to credit him with all the good qualities he had himself.

This day, Bozza, who was usually at work before the other apprentices, did not appear until an hour after sunrise. He was paler and more dejected than ever, more taciturn and sinister than they had yet seen him. He had not had a moment's rest. He had wandered all night, like an unhappy ghost, through the dark, angular streets. His hair fell in tangles on his hollow cheeks, his beard was disordered and bristling, and his black plume had been broken by the gale. He took his apron and tools in silence, and placed himself near Valerio, who was at work on his garland of the arch.

Francesco noticed the tardy arrival of his apprentice; but Bozza was always so prompt that the master refrained from alluding to this delinquency, the first of which he had been guilty during the three years of his apprenticeship.

Valerio, always outspoken, and actuated by a kindly solicitude, did not hesitate to question him.

"What is the matter, comrade?" said he, gazing at him with surprise from head to foot. "You look as if you had been buried overnight. Let me touch your hand to make sure that you are not your ghost."

Bozza pretended not to hear him, and did not respond to the offer of the friendly hand.

"You have been playing, eh, Bartolommeo? You lost money last night? Is that what ails you? Come, do not take the game to heart. If it is a question of money, don't let that trouble you. You know my purse is yours."

Bozza was silent.

"Oh, perhaps it is not that? Your sweetheart has deceived you, maybe, or you love her no longer, which is worse. Come, make a lovely Madonna to look like her, whose gentle eyes will be forever fixed on yours. Perhaps you have an enemy? Shall I act as your second in a duel? I am ready."

"You ask a good many questions, Messer Valerio," replied Bozza in a low but bitter tone. "Has it come to this, that for being an hour late your associates must submit to such catechising and give an account of their conduct?"

"Oh, oh!" cried Valerio, amazed, "you are in a very bad humor, my poor friend. It is to be hoped that when the paroxysm is past you will do more justice to my intentions."

He resumed his work, whistling the while, and Bozza began his with a deliberation and an affectation of indifference and awkwardness which Valerio did not wish to give him the satisfaction of noticing.

Nearly two hours went by, and Bozza, seeing he was not succeeding in irritating Valerio, changed his method, and began all at once to work rapidly, paying no attention to the materials he used, and mixing his colors in the oddest and most incongruous manner.

Valerio looked askance at him, and studied him for

some minutes. He was surprised at his obstinacy, but as it was the first time such a thing had happened he resisted the temptation which was goading him on to anger, and resolved to repair the work of his apprentice, saying to himself, "After all, it is only a day lost for him and for me."

But in spite of this generous resolution, and in spite of his determination not to cast his eyes on the execrable work to which Bozza was savagely devoting himself, the dry harsh sound of his *tampon* had something feverish and irritating in it, and the young master felt it was time to withdraw if he did not wish to show his temper. He was at ease in his conscience. Bozza's condition seemed to him a kind of distemper, calling more for pity than anger. Brave as a lion, but like the lion generous and patient, he left his scaffolding, donned his black silk doublet, and went to breathe the air for a moment in the court of the basilica adjoining the ducal palace, one of the most beautiful pieces of architecture in the world.

After making several turns under the galleries, he thought himself calm enough to go back to the studio, and as he descended the Giant's Staircase, he found himself all at once face to face with Bozza. The same kind of irritation that Valerio had felt while hiding his anger had rankled in Bartolommeo's heart while he was trying in vain to enkindle that of his rival. After Valerio had fled from his mute torture, his own had become so exasperating that he could no longer control it. Minutes seemed centuries to him, and, suddenly carried away by a feeling of irresistible hatred, he hastily followed in Valerio's footsteps, and joined him on the spot where, nearly two hundred years before, the head of Marino Faliero had rolled from the block. All Valerio's anger was roused again, and the two young artists, immovable, with flashing eyes, remained for several moments undecided, each waiting impatiently for the provocation of his adversary. They seemed like two fierce dogs, growling inaudibly, with bloodshot eyes and bristling backs, ready to spring upon each other.

VII.

DESPICABLE as were the artifices of Bianchini, the spirit of observation with which nature had endowed him, and the perfect knowledge he had of the weakness and follies of other men, served him better than the superiority of others would have done. He had a profound and inveterate hatred of the human race. Denying the existence of conscience, he detested everything resembling it. He did not shrink from any means of corruption. He never took into account the possibility of good intentions. His dark presentiments were almost always verified. But it is true to say, that, as the tempest breaks only those trees whose sap has begun to dry up and whose trunks have lost their elastic vigor, so the wicked schemes of Bianchini triumphed only over hearts where the feeling of love, the sap of life, flowed sparingly, and was choked at each effort by the violence of contrary passions. An instinctive cowardice prevented him from attacking strong and generous souls directly. He knew only the bad side of life, and this sinister knowledge made him bold in the practice of duplicity.

If he had dared to face Bozza with such a palpable lie, it was because he foresaw that the latter, being of a distrustful and self-centred nature, would not seek the elucidation of it. Bozza, without exactly liking deceit, hated frankness. His great failing was an extraordinary self-love, always being wounded, always suffering. Bianchini knew also that the whole effort of his will was to conceal this weakness,—that the fear of betraying it by his words made him silent, incapable of all expansion, an enemy to all explanations which could but lay bare the depths of his soul. If Bartolommeo sometimes half revealed himself to Francesco, it was because, seeing the melancholy of the latter, and thinking him afflicted with the same malady as himself, he feared him less than others. But he was deceived. Francesco's malady, with the same outward symptoms, was of a totally different nature from his own. His opinion of Valerio, as he did not understand him at all, was that he was a man made up of contradictions. He was convinced that all this naïve nonchalance was an habitual affectation, in order to win friends and adherents, and to make his way through the influence of those in power. It was owing to this misconception that the ruse of Bianchini had succeeded.

When Bozza came into the presence of Valerio, although he was not at all cowardly, his courage forsook him. His determination to reproach him for his supposed conduct of the night before gave way to the fear of showing how much his pride had suffered by that childish provocation. He felt that true dignity required him to ignore it, or to pretend to do so, and, instantly stifling his anger in the bottom of his heart, he assumed his cold and disdainful air.

Valerio, surprised at the sudden change in his manner and expression, broke the silence first by asking him what he had to say to him.

"I have to say to you, Messer," replied Bozza, "that you must look for another apprentice. I am going to leave your school."

"Because —" cried Valerio with the impatience of a frank open nature.

"Because I feel obliged to leave you," answered Bozza. "Ask me no more."

"And in announcing it to me so unexpectedly," said Valerio, "did you mean to wound me?"

"Not at all, Messer," replied Bozza in a chilling tone.

"In that case," said Valerio, making a great effort to control his temper, "you owe it to the friendship which I have always shown you to tell me the cause of your leaving."

"It is not a question of friendship, Messer," replied Bozza with a bitter smile. "That is a word which must not be thrown away, and a feeling which can exist but slightly between you and me."

"It may be that you have never felt it for any one," said Valerio, wounded, "but with me this feeling was sincere, and I have given you too many proofs of it for it to be becoming in you to deny it."

"You have indeed given me proofs of it," said Bozza ironically, "which it will be difficult for me to forget."

Valerio, astonished, looked at him fixedly. He could not believe in so much bitterness; the language of hatred he would not understand.

"Bartolommeo," said he, seizing his arm and leading him under the galleries, "you have something on your mind. I must have offended you involuntarily. Whatever it may be, I swear upon my honor that I would not have done it for anything. That I may convince you, tell me what it is."

There was so much sincerity in the young master's voice and manner that Bozza thought Bianchini must have been playing upon his credulity; but at the same time he felt more than ever the desire to conceal his inordinate sensitiveness, and the knowledge of his own weakness only made Valerio's generous candor the more humiliating to him. His heart, closed to affection, did not feel the need of responding to these advances. "If Bianchini has lied," said he to himself, "if Valerio does not despise me this time, he has despised me every day of his life, and he despises me this very moment by offering me his patronizing friendship and the forgiveness of a fault. Since I have gone so far as to say it, I shall have to go on." Indeed, for a long time Bozza had been uneasy in the society of the Zuccati, and had hoped to break away from it.

"You have never offended me, Messer," he answered coldly. "If you had done so, I should not be contented with leaving you; I should demand satisfaction."

"And in truth I am ready to give it to you if you persist in believing it," replied Valerio, who felt keenly the dissimulation of his apprentice.

"That is not the question, Messer; and to prove to you that, if I do not seek a quarrel, at least it is not through fear that I avoid it, I am going to tell you a reason for leaving you which may displease you a little."

"Let us have it," said Valerio. "We should always speak the truth."

"I wish to tell you, master," said Bozza, speaking in the most pedantic and wounding tone he could assume, " that this is a question of art and nothing more. Perhaps this may make you smile,— you who despise art. But as for me, who prize nothing else in the world, I must acknowledge to you that I am a man ready to sacrifice the pleasantest relations in life in order to make progress and speedily become a master."

"I do not blame you for that," said Valerio; "but in what way is your progress hindered by me? Have I neglected to teach you? And, instead of employing you, as masters are in the habit of doing, in the mechanical work of the school, have I not treated you like an artist? Have I not offered you all possible opportunities for advancing, confiding to you interesting, difficult work, and showing you the best method, as heartily as if you had been my own brother?"

"I do not deny your kindness," said Bozza; "but at the risk of seeming a little vain I must confess, master, that this method which seems the best to you does not satisfy me. I aspire not only to be first in my art, but still further to bring that art, incomplete in your hands, to a degree of perfection the revelation of which I feel within me. Therefore you will permit me to free myself from your method, and to follow my own. An inner voice compels me. It seems to me that I am destined for something better than to walk in the footsteps of others. If I fail, do not pity me. If I succeed, count upon me in my turn to refuse you neither my assistance nor my advice."

Valerio, not suspecting, so devoid was he of vanity, that this speech was invented for the sole purpose of annoying him profoundly, could scarcely keep from laughing. He had often noticed Bozza's extreme self-love, and at this moment it seemed to him he was suffering from an attack of mental aberration. It was thus that he accounted for the excited state in which he had seen him all the morning, and, realizing what a gloomy and misery-breeding state it was, he had the kindness not to ridicule him too openly.

"If that is the case, my dear Bartolommeo," said he smiling, "it seems to me that by remaining with us it would be easier for you to give us this advice and for us to receive it. As you have never been opposed in your work, nothing shall prevent you from improving and innovating as you choose. If you bring our art to a greater degree of perfection, I can promise you that, far from hindering it, I shall be glad to profit by it for my own sake."

Bozza felt that Valerio, in spite of his good nature, was making fun of him a little. In despair that he had in vain wished to be wicked, and had only made himself ridiculous, he could no longer control himself, and he answered him several times in a tone so bitter that Valerio lost all patience, and at last said to him: —

"Really, my dear friend, if the extraordinary and miserable work you were doing just now when I left the basilica is a revelation of your genius, I should much prefer that art should retrograde in my hands than make such progress in yours."

"I see, Messer," replied Bozza, vexed that all his little intrigues turned against himself, "you are not deceived by the excuses I have invented since morning for leaving you. I wanted to displease you, so that you might turn me away, thereby saving you the mortification of being left in the lurch. I am sorry you did not understand my disinterestedness in this matter, and have obliged me to tell you that I shall not remain an hour longer in your school."

"And the cause of your going must remain a secret?" said Valerio.

"No one has the right to ask me," answered Bozza.

"I could oblige you to fulfil your engagement," replied Valerio, "for I have your written contract to work under my direction until next St. Mark's; but I do not wish to be served by constraint. You are free."

"I am ready to indemnify you to any amount you may exact, Messer," replied Bozza, "for I fear nothing so much as to remain your debtor."

"You will have to be resigned to that, however," said Valerio, saluting him, "for I am determined to accept nothing from you."

So they parted, the master and the apprentice. Valerio watched him going, and walked nervously under the arcades. Then, suddenly overcome with sadness at the sight of so much ingratitude and obduracy, he returned to his work, his face bathed in tears.

Bozza, on the contrary, went to seek his sweetheart, and treated her better than usual that day. He was light-hearted, almost gay. He felt his soul relieved of a heavy load; it was the weight of gratitude, a feeling insupportable to the proud. He imagined he had just triumphed over all his past, and was entering with full sails into the glorious independence of the future.

VIII.

BOZZA was not an artist without merit. Not only was he very superior to the Bianchini, who were merely diligent and painstaking workmen, but he had received from the Zuccati advanced ideas in designing and coloring. His drawing was elegant and correct, his tone was not lacking in truth, and in rendering the brilliancy and richness of material he surpassed perhaps even Valerio himself. But if by dint of study and perseverance he had succeeded in producing mechanical effects, he was far from having drawn down from Heaven that sacred fire which gives life to the productions of art, and which constitutes the superiority of genius over talent. Bozza was too intelligent and too much in earnest in his search after the secret of this superiority in others not to understand what he lacked himself, and to seek diligently to acquire it. But in vain did he try to give to his characters the pathetic grace and lofty enthusiasm which distinguished those of the Zuccati. He succeeded in painting the physical emotion only. In the scene from the Apocalypse, the faces of the demons and the damned were very well handled. But although he excelled in this, he did not know how to give to these impersonations of hatred and misery the intellectual sentiment which ought to characterize religious pictures. The wicked did not seem to be tormented by the flames which consumed them. No feeling of shame or despair was portrayed in their features contracted by the heat. The rebel angels retained nothing of their celestial origin. Their regret at the loss of their primitive greatness was stifled under a frightful expression of irony, and in gazing at these immovable features, these wild grimaces, these tortures which recalled the Inquisition rather than the judgments of God, one was more startled than pained, more disgusted than awed.

In spite of these faults, perceptible only to superior natures, Bozza's work possessed excellent qualities, and the Zuccati well understood his power when they intrusted it to him; but when he essayed more lofty subjects, he completely failed. His majestic movements were rigid, his inspired faces were grimacing. In vain his angels spread their strong and luminous wing; their feet seemed everlastingly embedded in the cement, and their eyes had no other light than that of enamel or marble.

The disconcerted artists no longer recognized their own thoughts in the execution of their designs, however faithful in technique they might be; and the Zuccati were obliged to retouch with great care all which in their faces indicated feeling and the portrayal of moral life. From the time that the scene from the Apocalypse had been completed, Bozza had been employed on the grand festoon of the arch; and, as he had deemed it unworthy of his genius to be assigned the task of making a servile copy of ornamentation, he experienced interiorly all the tortures of wounded pride. It was nevertheless with extreme gentleness and delicacy that the Zuccati had made him feel the need of leaving sacred subjects to more able hands, and of finishing the details of the arch while waiting until subjects suited to his peculiar talent should be consigned to their school.

Bozza made no account of the special lessons in designing and painting which the Zuccati gave him in their leisure hours. To him nothing was of so much importance as his own future glory, and in his heart he reproached Valerio for his love of pleasure, which prevented him from devoting all his spare moments to him, and he reproached Francesco for a too close application to his own work, which sometimes obliged him either to shorten these lessons or to put them off until the following day. He flattered himself that these masters feared he would surpass them, and that they purposely deprived him of the means of advancing himself, in order that they might profit the longer by his work. So in his secret soul he abandoned himself to all the agony of jealousy and resentment.

At other times — and these moments were still more trying — he was forced to open his eyes and admit that, in spite of the excellent lessons and disinterested advice they had given him, he had not progressed as he should have done. He felt all the defects of his work keenly, and asked himself in dismay if, beyond a certain degree of talent, he was always to find himself baffled. He realized what he lacked, but could not attain it. His hand seemed to translate into commonplace words the poetic inspirations of his brain, and he half believed the infernal powers had some jealous designs on his destiny.

Valerio often said to him, "Bartolommeo, the greatest obstacle to the development of your faculties is the intense anxiety that preys upon your mind. Nothing beautiful or grand can blossom except under the fructifying breath of a warm heart and a free spirit. It requires all the health of body and soul to produce sound work; that which comes from a sick brain has not the conditions of life. If, instead of shedding the choking tears of weariness and discouragement, you would really cry with tenderness and sympathy on the bosom of a friend,—if, in fine, in those hours when you are so overcome with fatigue that you can neither hold your tools nor discern colors, sooner than weary your sight or allow your will to become paralyzed, you would seek in the diversions of your age, in the innocent sports of youth, a means of restoring the strength of the artist, giving it for a time a different treatment,—I think you would be surprised on resuming your work to feel your heart beat vigorously, and your whole being transported with an unknown joy and an invincible hope. But you seem in a manner determined to be always sad, and ready to sink at any moment under the burden of life. How can you give to your work that life that is not in yourself? If you continue in this way, all the resources of your genius will be exhausted before you can make them serve you. By dint of looking at the end, and of exaggerating the price of victory, you are hindered from experiencing the sweet emotion and pure delight of the work itself. Art, out of revenge for not being loved for herself alone, reveals herself only at a distance to your blurred and deceived vision; and if by resorting to unusual methods you happen to succeed in winning the vain applause of the crowd, you will not feel within you the noble satisfaction of the conscientious artist who can smile at the ignorance of crude judges, and console himself for his poverty by shutting himself up in a cot or a cave with his Muse, enjoying in her embrace an ecstasy unknown to the vulgar."

The unfortunate artist fully understood the truth of these words, but, instead of believing that Valerio addressed them to him in the simplicity of his soul, and with the sincere desire of placing him on the right track, he accused him of harboring a feeling of malicious pleasure and cruel contempt at sight of his misery. Discouraged and disheartened, he would then exclaim: "Yes, that is too true, Valerio. I am lost. I am consumed like a torch blown by the wind, without having thrown my light or filled my lamp. You know it, you have put your finger on the wound. You know the secret of your power and of my weakness. Triumph then, humiliate me, contemn my dreams, blast my hopes, laugh at my aspirations. You have known how to use your strength; you have controlled the race-horse; you have tamed him. As for myself, I spur him incessantly, and, being carried away by him, I go to pieces against the first obstacle."

It was in vain that the two Zuccati sought to pacify him and restore his hope. He repulsed their kindly interest, and, hurt by their compassion, he tried to hide his discomfort afar from all eyes and all consolation.

Seeing that their affectionate advice only served to aggravate the misery of this tortured soul, the two young masters at last ceased speaking with him about himself; and Bozza concluded thereby that they no longer loved him, and were afraid that perhaps he might profit too much by their advice. The unfortunate necessity of abandoning a noble and interesting work in order to finish some carefully selected ornamentation in a given time had ended by embittering him. He had then resolved to leave them as soon as his engagement should expire, for he had no hope that they would propose him for the mastership, as they had the right to do, according to the terms of their agreement with the Procurators. This right extended to only one pupil a year, and Ceccato and Marini, his young associates, seemed to him to be more in favor with the Zuccati than himself. He had an idea of going to Ferrara or to Bologna to engage himself as a master, and form a school; for if he was one of the last in Venice, he might hope to be one of the first in a city less wealthy and less renowned. His quarrel with Valerio had, in his eyes, the double advantage of rendering him free and of giving him an occasion for revenge.

The work was not finished, the feast of Saint Mark was drawing near, the moments were counted. In the two schools zeal was redoubled in order that they should not fall behind with their engagements. The absence or departure of one apprentice at this time would be a real loss, and would seriously compromise the success of the extraordinary efforts which were being made up to this day, in order not to be outdone by the rival school.

IX.

THE Bianchini were not slow to notice the absence of Bozza or the sadness of Valerio. Vincent, with a brutal smile, related his artifice of the evening before to his two brothers, and all three of them, encouraged by this first success, resolved to do everything in their power to injure the work in the grand cupola and to ruin the Zuccati. After consulting together at the tavern, Vincent put himself on Bozza's track, and discovered him early in the evening in the great orchard which extends along the border of the lagunes in the neighborhood of Santa Chiara. Bozza crept slowly along close to a stretch of greensward dotted with beautiful trees, whose branches leaned affectionately above the placid waters. A profound silence reigned over this rural city, and the last rays of the setting sun tinted faintly in the distance the rustic clock of the Isle of Certosa. On this side Venice presents an appearance as naïve and pastoral as on other sides coquettish, proud, or terrible. Here one sees only boats landing laden with fruit or vegetables; here one hears only the sound of the rake on the walk, or the hum of the spinning-wheels of the women seated in the midst of their children on the doorsteps of their fruit-houses. Here the convent clocks strike the hours in a tone clear and tender, and nothing interrupts the long melancholy vibration. It was here that in former days the author of "Childe Harold" often came to learn the meaning of certain mysteries of nature: grace, sweetness, charm, repose, strange words which nature, either powerless or pitiless in his regard, translated for him by languor, sadness, weariness, despair. Bozza, insensible to the soothing influence of such a charming evening, was absorbed in watching the rapid flight and bloody contests of the great sea birds, which at this hour quarrel over their last prey, or hurry to reach their hidden retreats. This wrestling and commotion was the only thing with which he was in sympathy. Everywhere the vanquished seemed to him the personification of his rivals; and when the conqueror flung upon the air his cry of rage and triumph, Bozza imagined himself mounting on huge wings to the goal of his insatiable desires.

Bianchini approached him with affected frankness,

and, after having told him that he had noticed for some time past the Zuccati's evil dealings with him, he begged him to tell him, under the seal of secrecy, if he had really decided to leave their school.

"There is no secret about it," answered Bartolommeo, "for it is not only a thing decided upon, but a thing done."

Bianchini expressed his pleasure with reserve, and assured Bozza that he might have stayed for ten years with the Zuccati without making any progress toward the mastership, and cited for example Marini, who was a talented fellow, and who had been with them for six years with no other recompense than a modest salary and the title of companion. "Marini flatters himself," he added, "that he will be made a master on St. Mark's Day, according to the promise of Messer Francesco Zuccati, but —"

"He promised it to him? Positively?" said Bozza, his eyes flashing.

"In my presence," answered Vincent. "Perhaps he made the same promise to you. Oh, there is no counting on the promises of the Zuccati. They treat their apprentices as they treat the Procurators, — more talk than work. They have fine words by which they explain to their dupes that art requires a long novitiate, and that an artist would die in his prime if he gave himself too soon to the caprices of his imagination; and that the greatest talents had failed because too quickly freed from the servile study of the model, etc. What don't they say? They learned by heart in their father's studio, when their father had a studio, five or six high-sounding words which they heard said to Titian or Giorgione, and now they consider themselves masters in painting, and talk like lords. Truly, it is so ridiculous that I do not understand why that great devil of yours in the Apocalypse — that piece of work so perfect, so fantastically rendered, so horned and so good-natured that I can never look at it without laughing — does not detach itself from the wall, and with his lion's tail come and box their ears when they say things so foolish and so out of place coming from them."

Although Bozza was hurt by this coarse praise given to his most important effort, to a figure which he had intended to render terrible, not grotesque, he felt a secret pleasure in hearing the Zuccati denounced and laughed at.

When Bianchini thought he had gained Bozza's confidence by salving his wound, he offered to take him into his school, and went so far as to promise him a much larger salary than that he received from the

Zuccati; but he was surprised at getting only a refusal for his answer, and at not seeing the slightest satisfaction flit over Bozza's face. He thought that the young man would let himself be bought over for the sake of greater pecuniary advantages. The Bianchini could not see in the life of an artist any other end, any other hope, any other glory, than money.

After having tried in vain to tempt him with offers still more brilliant, Vincent gave up the idea of entering into business relations with him, and, assuming the complacent air of a man wholly disinterested, he sought by flattering him and conversing with him to find out the reasons for his refusal and the secret desires of his ambition. This was not difficult. Bozza, this man so defiant and so reserved that the most sincere friendship could not draw from him an acknowledgment of his weakness, yielded like a child to the seductions of the grossest flattery. Praise was like fresh air to his lungs, without which he would suffer and die. When Bianchini saw that his whole ambition was to become a master, and to have the glories of the profession in its authority, its independence, its title, regardless of acquiring no profit for his pains and of suffering all privations for a long time to come, he felt a profound contempt for this ambition, less vile than his own, and would have laughed at him openly if he had not thought he could yet use him to the detriment of the Zuccati.

"Ah, my young master," said he, "you would command, and not serve! It would be very easy, I know, for a man so talented as yourself. Very well! Long life to you! You must be a master, but not in a miserable little provincial town, where you might toil for twenty years without being noticed. You must become a master here in Venice, on Saint Mark's Day, cutting out and filling the place of the Zuccati."

"That is easier said than done," replied Bozza. "The Zuccati are all-powerful."

"Perhaps not so much as you think," replied Bianchini. "Will you pledge me your word to trust in me and help me in all my plans? I will pledge you mine that in six months the Zuccati will be driven from Venice, and that we two, you and I, will be sole masters in the basilica."

Vincent spoke with so much assurance, and he was known as a man so persevering, so capable, and so fortunate in all his undertakings, — he had escaped so many dangers and repaired so many disasters where anybody else would have failed, — that Bozza was moved, felt a thrill of pleasure coursing through his veins, and the perspiration stood in beads upon his forehead, as if the sun from out the sea into which it had just sunken were shedding upon him its very hottest rays.

Bianchini, seeing him duped, took his arm and drew him along with him.

"Come," said he, "I want to make you see with your own eyes a sure way of getting rid of our enemies; but first you must take an oath that you will not be influenced by any feeling of foolish sensitiveness, and will do nothing to check my plans. Your testimony is absolutely necessary to me. Are you sure that you will not shrink from any of the consequences of the truth, however hard they may bear upon your old masters?"

"And where will these consequences end?" asked Bozza in surprise.

"With life only," answered Bianchini. "They will lead to exile, dishonor, and want."

"I will not lend myself to that," said Bozza, dryly, moving away from his tempter. "The Zuccati are honest men, after all, and I cannot carry spite so far as to hate them. Let me alone, Messer Vincent, you are a wicked man."

"It seems so to you," replied Vincent, wholly

unmoved by an appellation for which he had long since ceased to blush. "That scares you because you believe in the honor of the Zuccati brothers. It is very nice and very naïve on your part. But if one could make you see — I say, with your own eyes — that they are men of bad faith, who deceive the Republic, and defraud its treasuries by stealing their salary and adulterating their work, — if I could make you see it, what would you say? And if, having made you see it, I should summon you at the time and place to bear witness to the truth, would you do it?"

"If I should see it with my own eyes, I should say that the Zuccati are the greatest hypocrites and the most outrageous liars I have ever met; and if, in that case, I should be summoned to bear witness, I should do it, because they would then have treated me shamefully, and I have too much hatred for men who have the right to lord it over others not to abhor those who arrogate to themselves this right at the price of falsehood. They robbers and villains! I do not believe it; but I would like to, if only for the pleasure of telling them to their face, 'No, you have no right to despise me.'"

"Follow me," said Bianchini with a hideous smile; "night is upon us, and moreover we can enter the basilica at any time without exciting suspicion. Come, and if you are not chicken-hearted, before six months you will make a great yellow devil on the highest scaffolding in the basilica which will laugh louder than all the others, and which will be worth to you a hundred golden ducats."

Thus speaking, he glided away among the sweet-scented trees; and Bozza, treading with an uneasy step on the border of thyme and fennel, followed him tremblingly, like one on the verge of committing a crime.

X.

THE following day, Bozza was to be seen in the school of the Bianchini, working zealously in the chapel of Saint Isidore. Francesco, to whom his brother had given an exact account of the scene of the evening before, was so deeply wounded by this conduct that he begged Valerio not to make any further attempt to ascertain his motives. He suffered in silence, resenting more strongly an injury done to his beloved brother than if it had been done to himself alone, not being able to understand how one could resist the frankness and sweetness of any explanation given by Valerio. He pretended not to see Bozza, and from that day passed him by as if he had never known him. Valerio, who well knew that his brother had set his heart upon finishing his cupola, and who saw the annoyance caused him by Bozza's desertion, resolved to die at the work rather than not overcome this difficulty. Francesco was in delicate health. His proud and sensitive soul was beset with the fear of not fulfilling his engagements. It was not a question of his reputation as an artist alone, a reputation which he reproached himself for having cherished too much, since he found himself retarded for want of some one to do the mechanical work; it was a question of honor. He was not ignorant of the plots already attempted by the Bianchini to blacken his good name. When he had accepted this enormous task, his father, thinking it too much of an undertaking for the three years to which it was limited, had tried to dissuade them from it. Titian, believing that Valerio's pleasure-loving life and the poor health of the other would make the execution of it impossible, advised them many times to become reconciled with the Bianchini, and to ask of the Procurators a new arrangement. But the Bianchini, who in the beginning had formed part of the school of Francesco, had little talent and an insurmountable pride. On no account would Francesco have intrusted to them a work undertaken and carried on with so much care and love.

In order to explain how important it was that this master should not be behind for a single day, we must go back a little, and say that the basilica of St. Mark had been retouched during the preceding years by incompetent and unreliable workmen.

Considerable expense had only served to entertain a troop of dissipated artisans, whose work it was necessary to repair at a great cost. Father Alberto and Rizzo, first mosaic masters, had shown to the Procurators the necessity of observing some method in regard to the expense and the work. After many experiments it was finally agreed that Francesco Zuccato should be the head of the mosaic studio; and Vincent Bianchini, notwithstanding he had been banished for fourteen years under accusation of passing false money and for having committed several murders, — one, notably that of his barber, — had, thanks to the strength of his work and that of his two brothers, found protection in the person of the *Procurator-Cassiere*, who had placed him under the direction of the Zuccati. But, harmony being an impossibility between these two families, Francesco had asked permission to choose some other pupils, and he had obtained it. To put an end to the quarrels which this gave rise to, and to pacify the Procurator, who was interested in the Bianchini, the commission had decided to believe upon hearsay that the latter were capable of working without direction on their own account. To them was assigned a less favorable position and a longer task than to the Zuccati. They themselves had made these conditions, and asked this trial of their talents. From that time they had not ceased to make themselves important in the eyes of the commission, who were, moreover, anything but enlightened on the matter, and to depreciate the school of Francesco, whose modesty and candor would not allow him to argue against them. The commission felt themselves in honor bound to have work more elaborate and better done at less expense than in the past. They wished, at the opening of the renovated church, to deserve praise and remuneration from the Senate.

Francesco saw the fatal day approaching, and it was in vain he put forth all his strength; hope began to forsake him. He also saw that Valerio, insensible to care and anxiety, was determined to celebrate on that same day the organization of a company of men of pleasure. Bozza's withdrawal at such a critical moment bewildered him. "Even if," said he to himself, "Valerio should give all his time and strength to his work, it would not amount to much. Let him amuse himself, then, since he is so fortunate as to be insensible to the disgrace of failure."

But he was mistaken in Valerio, who knew too well his brother's chivalrous susceptibility not to

THE MASTER MOSAIC-WORKERS.

realize also that he would be inconsolable under such a mortification. Therefore he called together his favorite pupils, Marini, Ceccato, and two others. He explained to them the condition of Francesco's mind, and that of all the school, in the face of public opinion. He besought them to do like himself, — not to despair, not to give up either the work or the pleasure, but to remain at their post until all was successfully accomplished, even were they to perish the day after Saint Mark's. They all swore to stand by him without relaxation, and they kept their word. In order not to worry Francesco, who was always anxious on account of the little care Valerio took of his health, they covered up with planks that part of the work which he was reserving for his last touches, and worked upon it during the night. A light mattress was thrown upon the scaffolding, and when one of the workmen was overcome with fatigue, he stretched himself upon it and enjoyed a few moments' sleep, interrupted by the joyous singing of the others and the creaking of the planks under their feet. They took all their trouble in good part, and pretended that they had never rested better than when rocked to sleep by the scaffolding, and lulled by the sound of the hammer. Valerio's constant cheerfulness, his pleasant stories, his rollicking songs, and the great cruse of Cyprus wine which was passed around, kept up a wonderful enthusiasm. This devotion was crowned with success. On the eve of Saint Mark's, as the day was drawing to a close, and when Francesco, not wishing to give even a silent reproach to his brother, affected a resignation which he was far from feeling in his soul, Valerio gave the signal, the pupils took away the planks, and the master saw the festoon and the beautiful angels that supported it finished as if by magic.

"Oh, my dear Valerio!" cried Francesco, transported with joy and gratitude, "was I not inspired when I gave wings to your portrait? Are you not my guardian angel? my archangel deliverer?"

"I was very desirous," said Valerio, returning his caress, "to prove to you that I could attend to affairs of business and those of pleasure at the same time. Now, if you are satisfied with me, I am well paid for my pains; but you must also thank these courageous companions who have assisted me so kindly, and who have thereby made themselves worthy of the mastership. It is for you to choose, I do not say the most skilful, for they are all equal in that respect, but the oldest one entitled to it."

"My dear children," said Francesco, after cordially

embracing them, "you have all of late made generous sacrifices of your rights and of your wishes to supply the loss of a young man sick with ambition, whose talents and troubles seem to call for your interest and compassion. You had resolved among yourselves to prove to him that he accused you wrongfully of being his rivals and his enemies. Caring more for my instruction than for that vainglory with which he is consumed, you were on the point of giving him a grand example of virtue and disinterestedness, of making him a master voluntarily and against his expectations. The ungrateful fellow could not wait for this happy day, whereon he would have been forced to love and admire you. He has flown like a coward from masters whom he has not understood, and from comrades whom he has not appreciated. Forget him. Whoever loses you is sufficiently punished. Where shall he find friendships more sincere, services more disinterested? Now, one place of mastership is at your disposal because it is at mine, and I have no other wish than yours. God preserve me from making a choice among my pupils whom I esteem and love so tenderly! Make your own election. Whoever among you shall have the greatest number of votes shall have mine."

"We shall not be long deciding," said Marini. "We supposed, dear master, that you would do this year as in preceding years, and we have made our choice. Upon me has fallen the greatest number of the votes of the school, Ceccato has given me his, and I am elected. But all this is the result either of injustice or of misunderstanding. Ceccato works better than I. Ceccato has a wife and two little children. He has need of the mastership and a right to it. I am not pressed, I have no family. I am happy under your direction; I have yet much to learn. I transfer all my votes to Ceccato, and give him mine, to which I beg you, master, to add your own."

"Embrace me, brother," exclaimed Francesco, clasping Marini in his arms. "This beautiful act heals the wound which the ingratitude of Bartolommeo has made in my heart. Yes, there are still among us artists of great soul and noble devotion. Do not blush, Ceccato, in accepting this generous sacrifice. In Marini's place, we all know you would have acted as he has done. Be as proud as if you were the hero of the evening. Whoever inspires such a friendship is the equal of him who proves it."

Ceccato, all in tears, threw himself into Marini's

arms, and Francesco made it his duty to go at once to the Procurators, in order that they might ratify the promotion to the mastership due annually to one of the pupils, according to the terms of the contract passed between him and these magistrates.

"We will go and wait for you at table," said Valerio, "for after so much hard work we need some refreshment. Make haste to join us, brother, because I must go and spend half the night at San Filippo preparatory to the joyous festivities of to-morrow, and I do not wish to leave the supper table until I have clicked my glass with yours."

XI.

JUST as Francesco was ascending the grand staircase of the palace of the Procurators, he met Bozza, pale and absorbed in his thoughts, who was coming down. Finding himself face to face with his old master, Bartolommeo started, and was evidently ill at ease. As Francesco looked at him with a severity befitting this encounter, his face at once fell, and his pale lips moved as if vainly trying to speak. He stepped towards his master, and was about to salute him. Overcome with remorse, Bozza would have given his life could he at this moment have thrown himself at Francesco's feet and confessed all. But Francesco's cold recognition, the crushing look he cast upon him, and the pains he took to evade his salutation by turning away when he saw him lift his hand to his cap, left him without courage to seize this opportune moment for repentance. He stopped irresolutely, waiting for Francesco to turn and encourage him with a gentle look. Then seeing that he was decidedly condemned and deserted, "So be it," said he, clinching his fist with anger and despair. Then he strode away.

Francesco went first to the apartment of the *Procurator-Cassiere* who was the head of the commission. He was surprised to find Vincent Bianchini seated familiarly with him, and haranguing in a loud voice. But he was silent as soon as he saw Francesco, and went into an adjoining room. The *Procurator-Cassiere*, Melchior, frowned and affected an austere manner, to which his short, broad face, his round stomach and nasal utterance, gave a character more grotesque than imposing. Francesco was not a man, however, to be deceived by this professional trickery; he greeted him, and said he was happy to to be able to announce to him that the cupola was completed, and that consequently — But the *Procurator-Cassiere* did not give him time to finish his sentence.

"Well, well! at last!" said he, looking him full in the eye with the evident intention of intimidating him. "It is wonderful, Messer Zuccato, it is indeed. Will you have the goodness to explain to me how it was so quickly accomplished?"

"So quickly, Monsignore? It has been very slowly to my mind, for it is now the eve of the appointed day, and I was very much afraid this morning that it would not be done in time."

"And you had reason to be afraid, for yesterday a whole quarter of your festoon was yet unfinished, a task requiring about a month of ordinary labor."

"That is true," answered Francesco. "I see your Lordship has kept track of the least details."

"A man like me, Messer," said the Procurator emphatically, "knows the duties of his office, and does not allow himself to be imposed upon by such a man as you."

"A man like your Lordship," answered Francesco, surprised at this outburst, "ought to know that a man like me is incapable of imposing upon any one."

"Lower your voice, Messer, lower your voice," cried the Procurator, "or, by the ducal cap! I will make you hold your tongue for a long time."

The Procurator Melchior had the honor of counting among his great-uncles a Doge of Venice, so he had acquired the habit of thinking that he was a little doge himself, and always swore by his cap, which was made like a Phrygian bonnet or a cornucopia, the august insignia of the ducal dignity.

"I see that your Lordship is ill disposed to listen to me," answered Francesco, gently, with a little touch of disdain in his voice. "I shall withdraw for fear I might displease you further. I will wait for a more favorable moment—"

"To demand the salary for your laziness and deceitfulness," exclaimed the Procurator. "The salary of those who steal from the Republic is imprisonment, and take care that you are not rewarded according to your deserts."

"I am at a loss to know why you make me such a threat," answered Francesco. "I think your Lordship has too much wisdom and experience to take advantage of my present position, which will not allow me to resent an insult on your part. The respect due to your age and dignity closes my mouth, but I will not be so patient with the villains who have poisoned your mind against me."

"By the cap! this is not the place to play the bully, Messer. See that you justify yourself before accusing others."

"I will justify myself before your Lordship, and in a satisfactory manner, when you will condescend to tell me of what I am accused."

"You are accused, Messer, of having unworthily played upon the Procurators in passing yourself off for a mosaic-worker. You are a painter, and nothing else. Indeed, you are very talented in that, by the cap of my great-uncle! I congratulate you.

But you are not paid for making frescos, and we will see what yours are worth."

"I swear upon my honor that I have not the happiness to understand your Lordship's language."

"Sdeath! We'll make you understand, and until then you need not hope to receive any money. Ah! ah! *Mister* Painter, you were right when you said, 'Monsignore Melchior understands nothing of the work which we do. He is a good man, but much better employed in drinking than in directing the fine arts of the Republic.' All right, all right, Messer; we know all about your jokes and your brother's at our expense and that of the honorable body of magistrates. 'But he laughs best who laughs last.' We will see what a figure you will cut when we examine in person this beautiful work; and you will see that we know the difference between enamel and paint, pasteboard and stone."

Francesco could not repress a smile of scorn.

"If I clearly understand the accusation brought against me," he said, "I am guilty of having replaced some parts of the stone-work by painted pasteboard. It is true, I made something to resemble the Latin inscription which your Lordship ordered me to place above the outer door. I thought that your Lordship, not having taken the trouble yourself to prepare this inscription, too flattering for us, had intrusted it to some one who executed it in haste. I therefore took the liberty of correcting the word *Saxibus*, but, faithful to the duty I owe to the honorable Procurators, I traced the word in stone as I received it in writing from their hands, and allowed my brother to make the correction only on a piece of pasteboard glued to the stone. If your Lordship thinks that I am in fault, it is only a matter of taking away the pasteboard, and the text will appear beneath it executed to the letter, as can be plainly proved by your own eyes."

"Wonderful, Messer!" cried the Procurator, beside himself with rage. "You are convicting yourself. Here is a new proof of which I shall take note. Hollo! Secretary, set down this avowal. By the ducal cap! we will bring down your insolent pride. Ah! you think you can correct the Procurators! They understand Latin better than you do. Look you, what a scholar! Who would suspect he had such a variety of information? I will beg a chair for you as Professor of the Latin Language in the University of Padua, for surely you are too great a genius to devote yourself to mosaic work."

"If your Lordship keeps to your barbarism, I will go directly and take down my pasteboard," said Francesco, wholly out of patience. "All the Republic will know to-morrow that the Procurators cannot boast of their knowledge of Latin; but what does it matter to me?"

Speaking thus, he moved toward the door, while the Procurator cried to him imperiously to leave his presence, a command which he did not need to repeat, for he was no longer master of himself.

Scarcely had he left the chamber, when Vincent Bianchini, who had heard all in an adjoining room, entered hurriedly.

"Eh, Monsignore, what are you doing?" said he. "You gave him to understand that his fraud was discovered, and yet you let him go."

"What do you want me to do?" answered the Procurator. "I refused to pay him his salary, and I humiliated him. He is punished enough for to-day. After to-morrow we will prepare the case."

"And during these two nights he will slip into the basilica, and replace all the pieces of pasteboard with pieces of enamel, and so I shall appear to have made a false statement, and my devotion to the Republic will turn against me."

"And how would you have me prevent his wicked

designs?" said the bewildered Procurator. "I will have the church locked."

"You cannot do it. Being the vigil of St. Mark, the church will be full of people, and who knows by what means he could not enter the most strongly fortified place? And then he will join his companions, enter into an understanding with them, invent excuses— All is lost, and I am lost, if you do not punish him at once."

"You are right, Bianchini, he must be punished at once; but how?"

"Say the word, send two officers after him, he has not reached the foot of the stairs; throw him into prison."

"By the ducal cap! that idea did not occur to me. But, Vincent, isn't it rather severe, such an act of authority—"

"But, Monsignore, if you let him escape, he will make fun of you all his life, and his brother, the clever fellow, who is the favorite of all these young patricians so jealous of your power and wisdom, will not hesitate to joke—"

"You are right, dear Vincent," cried the Procurator, emphatically, striking the little bell that stood upon his desk. "The ducal dignity must be respected, for I am of the ducal family, you know?"

THE MASTER MOSAIC-WORKERS.

"And you will be Doge some day, I hope," replied Bianchini. "All Venice counts on saluting you with the cap on your head."

The officers were despatched. Five minutes later, poor Francesco, not knowing by virtue of what power nor in punishment for what crime, was led blindfolded across a labyrinth of galleries, courts, and staircases, toward the cell for which he was destined. He stopped for a moment during this mysterious journey, and, by the sound of water murmuring beneath him, he knew he was crossing the Bridge of Sighs. His heart stood still, and the name of Valerio escaped from his lips like an eternal farewell.

XII.

VALERIO waited for his brother at the tavern until the moment when, urged by the young people who went there to find him, he was obliged to give up the hope of drinking with him and with the new master, Ceccato, that evening. Burdened with a thousand cares, weighed down with a thousand responsibilities for the fête of the morrow, he passed half the night running from his studio in San Filippo to the Place St. Mark, where arrangements were being made for the game of rings, and from there to the different workmen and manufacturers whom he employed for this occasion. Wherever he went, he was accompanied by his stanch apprentices, and many other young men of different callings who were deeply attached to him, and whom he engaged to carry messages from place to place. When the waggish band drew up in marching 'order, it was to the tune of song and laughter, joyous preludes of the morrow's festivities.

THE MASTER MOSAIC-WORKERS.

Valerio did not enter his lodging until three o'clock in the morning. He was surprised not to find his brother there; however, he did not give himself any unreasonable anxiety on that account. Francesco had a little love affair which he neglected when art, his favorite passion, required all his time, but for which he generally managed to absent himself whenever his work allowed him a little respite. Moreover, Valerio was not much inclined by nature to foresee evil, the very fear of which wears out the greater part of humanity. He went to sleep, reckoning on finding his brother in the morning, either at San Filippo or where the first meeting of the gay companions of the Lizard was to take place.

All the world knows that in the halcyon days of her splendor the Republic of Venice, in addition to the numerous corporations constituted to maintain her laws, counted in her midst private associations approved by the Senate, devout societies encouraged by the clergy, and pleasure organizations tolerated and even flattered in secret by a government anxious to encourage by its love of pleasure the industry of the working classes. The devout confraternities were often composed of people representing but one trade or profession, as that of merchants, tailors, gunners, etc. Others were made up of

THE MASTER MOSAIC-WORKERS.

various workmen or merchants of the same parish, who called themselves by its name, as that of St. John the Beggar, the Madonna of the Garden, St. George in the Seaweed, St. Francis of the Vineyard, etc. Each society had a building, called its studio (*scuola*), which was decorated at the common expense with works of the greatest masters in painting, sculpture, and architecture. These studios were composed generally of a lower room, called *l'albergo*, where the members assembled, a rich stairway, which was in itself a sort of museum, and a vast hall where Mass was said and where they held their conferences. There are still many studios in Venice which the government has preserved as monuments of art, or which have become the property of private individuals. That of St. Mark is to-day the museum of the paintings of the city That of St. Roch contains many masterpieces of Tintoretto and other illustrious masters. The mosaic pavements, the ceilings loaded with gold or ornamented with frescos by Veronese or Pordenone, the wainscoting sculptured in wood or engraved in bronze, the minute and dainty bas-reliefs in which the entire life of Christ or of some favorite saint is executed in white marble with inconceivable finish and detail, — such are the vestiges of that power and richness to which aristocratic republics can attain, but under which they must inevitably perish.

Moreover, each society or confraternity had its patronal feast, called *sagra*, on which occasions it appeared in all its splendor, and had the privilege of taking part in all the feasts and solemnities of the Republic, decorated with the insignia of the association. In the procession of St. Mark, they held the rank of parishioners, that is, they walked behind the clergy from their church, carrying their reliquaries, crosses, and banners, taking their places in chapels reserved for them during the ceremonies. The pleasure societies did not enjoy the same privileges, but they were permitted to repair to the great square, to erect their tents there, and to carry on their jousts and banquets. Each company took its title and its emblem according to its fancy, and met wherever it pleased. Some were composed of noblemen only, others admitted noblemen and plebeians indiscriminately, thanks to that apparent fusion of classes which we see in Venice to-day. The old paintings have preserved to us the elegant and picturesque costumes of the Company of the Stocking, who wore one red stocking and one white, the rest of the dress being made of a variety of the most brilliant colors. The Company of St. Mark wore a golden lion on the breast; that of St. Theodosius, a silver crocodile on the arm, etc.

Valerio, celebrated for his exquisite taste and ready skill at inventing and executing things of this kind, had ordered and directed everything pertaining to the exterior ornamentation, and it may be said that in this respect the Company of the Lizard eclipsed all the others. He had chosen this climbing animal for their emblem, because all classes of artisans, who composed their best members, — architects, sculptors, glaziers and painters on glass, mosaic-workers, and fresco-painters, — were, by the nature of their work, accustomed to climb, and to live, after a fashion, suspended to the walls of the arches.

On the Feast of Saint Mark, 1570, according to Stringa, and 1574, according to others, the immense procession made the circuit of the Place St. Mark under the tents in the arcades purposely erected in the form of arches outside of the arcades of the *Procuraties*, which were too low to admit the enormous crosses of solid gold, the huge chandeliers, the shrines of lapis-lazuli surmounted with lilies cut in silver, the reliquaries terminating in pyramids of precious stones, — in a word, all that luxuriant pageantry of which priests are so jealous and the common people of the corporations so vain. No sooner was the religious chant lost within the spacious vestibule of the basilica, while children and poor people busied themselves picking up the drops of perfumed wax which had fallen upon the pavements from thousands of tapers, and sought eagerly for any stray stones or pearls which might have escaped from the sacred jewels, than there appeared in the centre of the place as if by magic a large circle surrounded by wooden galleries, gracefully decorated with variegated festoons and silken draperies, beneath which the ladies could sit sheltered from the sun and watch the games. The pillars which supported the galleries were covered with waving banners, upon which were romantic mottoes in the naive and sprightly dialect of Venice. In the midst stood a colossal pillar in the form of a palm tree, upon the trunk of which were crawling a crowd of charming lizards, in gold, silver, green, blue, and striped, infinitely varied. From the top of the tree a beautiful fairy with white wings leaned towards this agile group, extending to it a crown in each hand. At the foot of the trunk, upon a crimson velvet platform, beneath a dais of brocade garnished with the most ingenious arabesques, was seated the queen of the feast, the giver of prizes, — little Marie Robusti, the daughter of Tintoretto, a beautiful child ten or twelve years of age, whom Valerio took pleasure in calling playfully his lady love, to whom he showed the most tender care and courteous attentions. When the galleries were filled, she appeared, dressed after the manner of Giambellino's angels, in a white tunic, with a veil of sky-blue and a delicate wreath of young vine on her beautiful fair hair, which fell in a thick golden mass about her alabaster neck. Messer Orazio Vecelli, Titian's son, gave her his hand. He was dressed in oriental costume, for he had come from Byzantium with his father. He seated himself near her, as did also a numerous group of young men distinguished by their talent or their birth, for whom places of honor had been reserved on the steps of the platform. The galleries were filled with the most brilliant ladies, escorted by gallant cavaliers. In a large reserved enclosure many prominent persons did not disdain to take their places. The Doge had set them the example. He accompanied the young Duke of Anjou, who was to become Henry III., King of France, and who was then passing through Venice. Luigi Mocenigo (the Doge) had it at heart to do him the honors of the city, and to display before his eyes, accustomed to the more austere pastimes and barbarous festivals of the Sarmatians, the dazzling luxury and enchanting gayety of the beautiful youth of Venice.

When all were seated, a purple curtain was raised, and the glittering Company of the Lizard came forth from a tent closed until then. They formed a solid phalanx, having at their head musicians dressed in the grotesque costumes of ancient times, and in the centre was their leader, Valerio. They advanced in good order until opposite the Doge and the Senators. There the ranks parted, and Valerio, taking from the hands of the standard bearer the red satin banner, on which shone a silver lizard, came forward, and, on his bended knee, saluted the Chief of the Republic. There was a murmur of admiration at the sight of this beautiful young man, whose strange and magnificent costume showed to advantage his elegant and graceful proportions. His tight-fitting green velvet coat with large slashed sleeves was open at the breast, revealing a corslet made of a kind of goods from Smyrna with a gold foundation covered with flowers in silk admirably shaded. He wore on his left thigh the escutcheon of the company, representing the lizard, embroidered with fine pearls on a crimson velvet ground. His belt was a masterpiece of arabesque, and his poniard, studded with stones, was the gift of Messer Tiziano, who had brought it to him from the East. A superb white plume, fastened to his cap by a diamond clasp, fell behind to his waist, and swayed with his movements as gracefully as the majestic aigrette of the Chinese pheasant, which rises and falls at every step.

For a brief moment an expression of joy at such success and the naïve pride of youth shone upon the animated face of the young man, and his sparkling eyes wandered over the galleries and caught all glances fastened upon himself. But soon this furtive joy gave place to a dark foreboding. His eyes anxiously sought anew some one in the crowd, but could not find him. Valerio stifled a sigh and returned to his phalanx, where he remained preoccupied, insensible to the gayety of others, deaf to the noise of the fête, his face darkened by a heavy cloud. Francesco, in spite of the promise he had made him to present the standard to the Doge himself, had not appeared.

XIII.

THE brilliant phalanx of the Company of the Lizard marched three times round the circle, amid the wild applause of the people, who were amazed, not without reason, at the beautiful costumes and fine appearance of all the young champions. According to the statutes of the company, it was necessary in order to become a member to be of a certain height, to have no deformity, to be under forty years of age, to come of an honest family, and consequently not to show any of those signs of hereditary degradation which perpetuate the stigma of original vice, from generation to generation, in the form of physical ugliness. Each candidate was obliged to give proof of good health, frankness, and loyalty, by drinking copiously on the day of approval. Valerio had it for a maxim that a good workman ought to be able to drink wine without becoming intoxicated, and that an honest man should have no fear for his reputation, nor for that of his neighbor, through a candor forced out of him by drunkenness. Certain statutes of this jovial confraternity are curious enough to be recorded here.

"No one shall be admitted who cannot drink six measures of Cyprus wine without falling into idiocy.

"No one shall be admitted who, at the seventh measure, babbles anything to the detriment of a friend or a companion.

"No one shall be admitted who, at the eighth measure, shall reveal the secret of his loves, and tell the name of his sweetheart.

"No one shall be admitted who, at the ninth measure, will betray the confidence of a friend.

"No one shall be admitted who, at the tenth measure, does not know enough to stop and refuse to drink."

It is difficult to determine to-day what this measure of Cyprus wine was; but if we judge by the weight of the armor which they carried to battle, the formidable samples of which are still in our museums, we must believe that they would make the most intrepid drinkers of to-day recoil.

Like their chief, the Companions of the Lizard wore a green doublet; the rest of the dress was white and close fitting, but their waistcoats were of yellow silk, their plumes were scarlet, and they carried a black and silver shield.

When the company had sufficiently promenaded and displayed their costumes and banners, they re-entered their tent, and twenty span of horses appeared in the arena. The introduction of these noble animals in their feasts was a luxury highly appreciated in Venice, and, as if the idea formed of them by a people little accustomed to seeing them could not be satisfied by the reality, they were metamorphosed by the aid of very grotesque paraphernalia into fantastic animals. Their coats were painted, and false tails, either of foxes, bulls, or lions, were fastened to them. The heads of some were decorated with birds' feathers or golden horns, or with masks of fabulous animals. Those belonging to the Companions of the Lizard were more beautiful than the others, and therefore were less foolishly transformed than was the custom at this time. Nevertheless, some of them were disguised as unicorns, by a long silver horn attached to the front of their bridles; others had glittering dragons or stuffed birds upon their heads. All of them were painted, some rose-color, some turquoise-blue, apple-green, or scarlet; some were striped like zebras or spotted like panthers; and others were covered with golden scales resembling the great fishes of the sea. Each span, similarly caparisoned, entered the lists, led by a Moretto, or little black slave, grotesquely dressed, and walking between the two quadrupeds, which caracoled pleasingly at the sound of the trumpets and the shouts of enthusiasm.

Valerio alone, influenced by the laws of a purer taste, appeared on a Turkish horse as white as snow, and of remarkable beauty. He had only a simple housing of tiger skin, and broad silver bands served him as reins. His mane, long and silky, mixed with silver threads, was twisted into tresses, and each tress terminated with a beautiful pomegranate flower cut in silver and of exquisite workmanship. His hoofs were silvered, and his full magnificent tail swept freely against his generous flanks. Like his master, he wore the ensign of the company, a silver lizard on a crimson ground, painted with extreme care on the left haunch; and, as he had the honor of carrying the chief, he was the only horse decorated with the escutcheon.

Valerio had the horses uncoupled, and, placing himself at the foot of the platform where sat little Marie Robusti, he manifested his approval of ten merry companions who offered to sustain the challenges, and who, mounting on their horses, placed themselves five at his right, and five at his left. Then the young Moors walked the other ten unmatched horses around the arena again, waiting until the ten champions taken from the people should present themselves for the race. They had not long to wait, and the games began.

After having run at the ring, and gained and lost the prize alternately, other young men came from the galleries and presented themselves to take the place of the losers, while other Companions of the Lizard replaced those from their lists who had been vanquished. The games went on in this way for some time. The chief remained all the while on horseback, presiding over the sports, going and coming, and far more frequently entertaining himself with his dear little Marie, who besought him in vain to take part in them, for it was to him alone, she said, she wished to give the grand prize. Valerio had superior skill in all these exercises, of which he scorned to make a parade. He preferred to direct and keep up the pleasure of his companions. Moreover, he was sad and preoccupied. He did not understand how it was, that, after the proof of devotion he had given his brother by finishing his work, he should push his austerity to the point of not assisting at the fête even as a spectator.

THE MASTER MOSAIC-WORKERS.

But Valerio awoke from his reverie when the three Bianchini descended into the arena, and asked to compete with the best racers in the company. Dominique Bianchini, called Rosetto (the Red), was a very good horseman. He had lived for a long time in other countries than Venice, in which city horsemanship was but little understood. All the Companions of the Lizard were not good riders. Only those who had been brought up in the country, or who were strangers in the city, knew how to manage the bridle and to sit upright in the saddle, a thing far less easy than a Venetian gondola. Three of the most expert presented themselves against the Bianchini, and were vanquished at the first round; then others succeeded them with the like result. The honor of the company was at stake. Valerio felt it, for, until then, the cavaliers had had the advantage over all the young men of the city, and even over the noble lords who had not disdained to compete with them. But his heart was so sad that he did not care to accept the challenge, and bring down the pride of the Bianchini. Vincent, seeing his indifference, and attributing it to the fear of being vanquished, cried to him with the voice of a bricklayer: —

"Hollo! eh, Monsignore, Prince of the Lizards,

are you changed into a tortoise, and do you find no more champions to oppose us?"

Valerio made a sign, and Ceccato and Marini advanced.

"And you, Signore Valerio, royal Lizardee," cried in his turn Dominique the Red, "do you not condescend to risk yourself with an antagonist so insignificant as myself?"

"Immediately, if necessary," answered Valerio. "Let your brothers try first with my two companions, and if they are beaten, I will give you a chance."

The two Bianchini were again victorious; and Valerio, determined not to leave them in the ascendant, at last set spurs to his horse, and threw him into a gallop. The trumpets blazed forth with sounds more proud and joyous, when he was seen swift as lightning making the circuit of the arena three times without deigning to raise his arm or look at the mark; and suddenly, when he seemed to be thinking of something else and acting like one preoccupied, he carried off the five rings, with a nonchalant and disdainful air. The Bianchini, as yet, had taken but four; they were, moreover, fatigued, and, as they had won until then, their defeat was not calculated to cause them much shame. But Rosetto, who had not taken part in the last contest, and who had been resting for some moments, was burning with the desire to humiliate Valerio. He felt a particular hatred for him, especially since Valerio had prevented his being received into the Company of the Lizard on account of his repulsive ugliness. Vincent, his elder brother, had been refused admission for having committed a dishonorable act, and for having gone through a damaging lawsuit. Gian Antonio alone had been admitted on trial; but he had not been able to drink three measures of wine without losing his head and insulting in words several very respectable people. All three of them found themselves excluded from the company in a very mortifying manner, and in order to avenge themselves they had made Bozza believe that he had been rejected beforehand because he was a bastard, and thus they prevented him from trying to enter their ranks.

Dominique darted toward Valerio, who wished to return to his place, and leave the game to the others.

"You promised me a chance to revenge myself, Don Lizard," said he. "Do you already withdraw from the game?"

Valerio turned, looked at Dominique with a contemptuous smile, and entered the arena without honoring him with any other answer.

"Begin, since you are winning," said Dominique. "Honor to whom honor is due."

Valerio darted forward and secured four rings, but what did not happen to him once in a hundred times happened at the fifth ring: he let it fall upon the ground. He had been startled by the face of his father, which had suddenly appeared in one of the near galleries. The old Zuccato seemed worried. He sought the eyes of Francesco, and the stern look he gave Valerio seemed to ask him, as formerly a mysterious voice asked Cain, "What hast thou done with thy brother?"

The Bianchini uttered a cry of joy. They felt sure they would be avenged by Dominique, but the proud precipitation with which he finished his course betrayed him; he missed the fourth ring. Valerio was conqueror. Under any other circumstances this victory would not have satisfied his self-esteem, but he was so anxious to close the games and go in search of his brother that he drew a long breath when commanded to advance and receive the prize. Already Marie's little hands held out to him the embroidered scarf, and he was preparing to dismount amid shouts of congratulations, when Bartolommeo Bozza, dressed in black from head to foot, his cap ornamented with an eagle's plume, appeared in the arena so suddenly that he seemed to have come out of the earth. He asked to take sides with the Bianchini.

"I have had enough of it; the game is finished," said Valerio testily.

"Since when," cried Bozza in a sharp and satirical tone, "did a chief of the arena draw back at the last moment through fear of losing a prize illy won? According to the very terms of the game you owe Messer Dominique a chance to rataliate, for he was evidently distracted during his last turn; moreover, he was very tired, and you ought not to be. Come on! If you are not as cowardly and fugacious as the lizard, your emblem, you are bound to give me a chance."

"I will give you that chance," replied Valerio angrily, "but this evening or to-morrow you will give me one of a more serious kind for the manner in which you have dared to speak to me. Come, begin. I throw up my hand, and give you three points."

"I do not want even one," cried Bozza. "Quick! a horse! What! this sorry jade!" said he, turning towards the Moor who offered him a mettlesome steed. "Have n't you a fresher one?"

So saying, he threw himself upon the horse with surprising agility, without putting his foot in the stirrup, and made him rear and caracole with such audacity that everybody was impressed in his favor. Then he darted like lightning into the course.

"I never play for less than ten rings," he shouted in an arrogant tone.

"All right, ten rings!" said Valerio, whose troubled look began to shake the confidence of his partisans.

Bozza brought down the ten rings at a single round; then, suddenly checking his horse at the height of his speed, after the daring and powerful manner of the Arabs, he leaped to the ground while the animal reared again, flung his weapon into the middle of the arena, and went to throw himself carelessly at the feet of Marie Robusti, casting a look of freezing irony upon his adversary.

Valerio, wounded to the quick, felt his courage rekindled. He had eleven rings to take in order to win. He was capable of doing it, but it was not exactly what he was in the habit of doing; for the games were rarely more than five, and Bozza must have practised considerably to meet with such success all at once. Nevertheless, contempt and resentment gave strength to the young master. He started, and made nine rings easily; but, when about to take the tenth, he was conscious that he trembled, and struck spurs to his horse in order to hide it and to have a chance to recover himself.

"Well, well!" said a voice in a neighboring gallery.

It was the voice of old Zuccato; it seemed to say, "You lose time, Valerio, and your brother is in danger." At least so Valerio thought, for his mind was bewildered. He turned his horse, and made the tenth ring.

Bozza grew pale. One ring more, and he was vanquished; but this would decide it, and Valerio was plainly excited. However, pride fought with this interior terror, and he would assuredly have won if Vincent Bianchini, seeing his triumph imminent, and finding himself near enough to make himself heard, had not said to him, while flinging upon him a look of malediction:—

"Yes, play, win, enjoy yourself, rampant beast! you will soon crawl under the leads with your brother!"

At the moment he uttered these last words, Valerio threaded the ring; he turned pale as death, and let it fall. Shouts arose from all sides; the companions and all the partisans of the Bianchini yelled with wild and insolent joy.

"My brother!" cried Valerio, "my brother under the leads! Who is the wretch that says so? Who has seen my brother? Who can tell me where he is?"

But his cries were lost in the uproar, order had fled. Bozza received the prize, and went his way, carried in triumph by the school of the Bianchini, to which was added a train of malcontents who had been refused admission into the Company of the Lizard. A thousand vulgar jests, a thousand blood-thirsty threats burst forth from that boisterous crowd. The terrified ladies clung to the scaffoldings to let the rabble pass. The Companions of the Lizard would have drawn their swords and fallen upon them. The officers and halberdiers had great trouble to restrain them. The crowd flocked in sympathy about the beautiful Valerio, in whom all the world, and we may well say all the women, were intensely interested. Little Marie cried, and angrily threw her crown under the horses' feet. In this riotous disorder Valerio, insensible to his defeat, and tortured with misgivings regarding his brother, ran this way and that, with bewildered looks, asking for his brother of every one he met.

XIV.

"WHAT are you dreaming about, master?" said Ceccato, joining him in the midst of the crowd, and seizing him by the arm. "How is it that you allow yourself to be so much disturbed by a cowardly, insolent word? Don't you see that Bianchini sprung this wicked trick upon you to make you miss the ring? He ought to be punished. But if you abandon your companions, if you sadden the fête by your absence, the Bianchini will triumph. It is easy to understand that they did it all in order to be avenged for their expulsion. Come, Master, lead back the little queen, and take a turn on the quays with the music. The Company cannot march without their head. At vespers we will look for Messer Francesco."

"But where can he be?" said Valerio, clasping his hands. "Who knows what they may have invented in order to throw him into prison?"

"In prison? It is impossible, Master! By what

right and under what pretext? Can a man be thrown into prison on the first accusation?"

"Nevertheless, he is not here. It must be some very serious cause that detains him. He knows that I cannot be happy at this feast without him, and, although he does not like fêtes, he owes me this mark of appreciation, this reward for my work. It must be that our enemies have lured him into some hiding place, assassinated him perhaps! Vincent Bianchini is capable of everything."

"Master, you are crazy; for the love of Heaven, come back to us! See, our discouraged phalanx is dispersing, and, if we do not redeem ourselves in the regatta this evening, the Bianchini will make such a talk about it that all Venice will be asking to-morrow, 'How about that grand fiasco of the Company of the Lizard?'"

Valerio allowed himself to be reassured a little by the thought that perhaps Francesco had been to see his father, and had been detained by him. The oddity and severity of old Zuccato justified this supposition up to a certain point, and the look of displeasure he had given Valerio made him think that he had come to censure him. He tried, therefore, to join his father in the crowd, prepared to endure his bitter jests, of which, in spite of his

THE MASTER MOSAIC-WORKERS.

tender feeling for his son, the old man was very prodigal; but he could not find him. Moreover, surrounded by his disconcerted companions, he was forced, if he would not have them entirely disband and renounce their festival day, to march at their head on the grand border of the Canal Saint George, which is to-day the Quay of the Great Slaves.[1]

The lively sound of the instruments, the gayety, a trifle proud and spiteful, of little Marietta, whom four companions carried in a sort of palanquin elegantly decorated with flowers, and with bands and arabesques designed by Valerio, the admiration of all the people in the lagunes and all the sailors of the port assembled on the bank and upon the floating piers, the noise and commotion served, in a measure, to reanimate Valerio. He renewed the hope of finding his brother during vespers, for which the first bell had sounded, calling for a pause in the festivities, when the sheath of a poniard fell from the roof of the ducal palace to his feet. Struck with a sudden conviction, he seized it, and drew from it a note written with a stub of charcoal, which by good fortune Francesco had found in his pocket.

"Companions who pass the day in joy to the

[1] Riva degli Schiavoni.

sound of trumpets, tell Valerio Zuccato that his brother is under the leads, and expects him." The note contained nothing more. Hearing the music approach, and fearing to let it pass, Francesco, who could see nothing, but who knew Valerio's favorite march played by the hautboys, had not taken time to finish his thought, but had thrown his warning through a little slit in the top of the walled windows, which, according to masonry, are justly called *jour de souffrance*.

Valerio uttered a frantic cry, and Francesco, in spite of the din of the instruments and the noise of the crowd, heard him in a voice of thunder pronounce these words: —

"My brother under the leads! Woe, woe to those who have put him there!"

Valerio stopped short with such an energetic movement that a whole army could not have moved him. The entire company halted spontaneously. The fatal news spread instantly through all the ranks, and they dispersed, some to follow Valerio, who darted like lightning under the arcades of the palace, others to find the Bianchini and force them to reveal the meaning of their behavior.

Valerio was running along, carried away by anger and grief, without knowing whither he was going.

THE MASTER MOSAIC-WORKERS.

But, obedient to I know not what instinct, he entered the court of the ducal palace. At this moment the Doge was ascending the Giants' Staircase with the Duke of Anjou, the Procurators, and some of the Senators. Valerio dashed boldly into the midst of all these magnificent lords, and, forcing his way, threw himself at the feet of the Doge, and seized his ermine mantle.

"What is the matter, my child?" said Mocenigo, turning towards him kindly. "Whence comes it that your beautiful face wears a look of despair? Have you been subjected to injustice? Can I repair it?"

"Your Highness," cried Valerio, pressing to his lips the hem of the ducal mantle, "yes, I am subjected to a great injustice, and my heart is broken with grief. My elder brother, Francesco Zuccato, the best mosaic artist in all Italy. the bravest champion and most loyal citizen of the Republic, has been thrown into prison, without your order, without your permission, and I come to ask you for justice."

"In prison! Francesco Zuccato!" exclaimed the Doge. "Who could have inflicted so severe a punishment on so noble a young man and so worthy an artist? If he has committed a fault deserving punishment, why was I not informed of it? Who gave the order? Which of you, gentlemen, will give me an account of this?"

No one answered. Valerio spoke again.

"Your Highness," said he, "the Procurators who had charge of the works in the basilica ought to know. Monsignore Melchior, the *Cassiere*, certainly ought to know."

"I will find out, Valerio," answered the Doge. "Take heart, justice shall be done. Let us pass."

"Your Highness, strike me with the hilt of your sword if my boldness offends you," said Valerio, without relinquishing the mantle of the Doge, "but listen to the plea of the most faithful of your citizens. Francesco Zuccato could not commit a fault. He is a man who never had so much as an evil thought. To put him in prison is to do him an injury for which he will never be consoled, and of which the whole city will be informed in an hour, if you do not set him free, if you do not allow him to show himself with his companions to all the public, who are surprised not to have seen him appear at their head. Yet again, your Highness, hear me. Francesco is as frail in body as the reed in the lagune. Let him pass but one day more in prison, and he might as well never come out; and you will have lost the best artist and best citizen of the Republic; and misfortune will come of it, for I swear —"

"Silence, child," interrupted the Doge, gravely. "Do not make foolish threats. I cannot set a prisoner free without the consent of the Senate, and the Senate will not give it without inquiring for what he was committed; for some grave suspicion must rest on a man's head if they put him in prison. I have promised you justice; do not doubt the Father of the Republic, but prove yourself worthy of his protection by wise and prudent behavior. All that I can do to lessen your anxiety and your brother's trouble is to allow you to go to him, that you may take care of him if his health requires it."

"I am grateful, your Highness. May you be blessed for this permission," said Valerio, bowing his head and relinquishing the mantle of the Doge, who went on his way.

The Duke of Anjou paused before Valerio, and said to him with a gracious smile: "Young man, take courage. I promise to remind the Doge that he has pledged himself to grant you speedy redress, and if your brother resembles you, I do not doubt he is a gallant knight and a loyal subject. I wish you to understand that, in spite of your failure,

I consider you the hero of the game, and I am so much interested in your appearance and your marked ability that I would like to take you to the court of France when the noble Republic of Venice will no longer require your services."

Speaking thus, he took off his rich golden chain and placed it on Valerio's neck, requesting him to keep it in remembrance of him.

XV.

VALERIO was conducted by two halberdiers to his brother's cell.

"And you too!" cried Francesco. "The wretches have got the better of you too, my poor child? What good has it done you to be without ambition and without vanity? Holy modesty, they have not respected thee any more!"

"I am not a prisoner by the will of the wicked," answered Valerio, clasping him in his arms, "but by my own wish. I shall never leave you. I come to share your straw bed and your black bread. But tell me, who brought you here, and on what accusation?"

"I don't know," answered Francesco, "but I am not surprised. Are we not in Venice?"

Valerio tried to console his brother, and to assure him that he could not have been arrested but through some mistake, and that he would be set at liberty at the earliest opportunity. But Francesco answered him with deep despondency:—

"It is too late now. They have done me all the evil they could do me. They have done me an injury which nothing can wipe out. What does it matter to me henceforth whether I remain a year or a day in this frightful prison? Do you think that I have felt the heat, do you think that I have felt bodily pain during this endless day? No, but I have suffered all the agony of the soul. I to be ranked with knaves and impostors! I, who, after so many long vigils and such conscientious work, so much zeal and devotion to the glory of my country, who to-day should have been crowned and carried in triumph by my school amid the applause of a grateful people, see me here in prison, as Vincent Bianchini was for assassination and for passing false money. This is the fruit of my labors, the recompense of my courage! Be a conscientious artist; apply yourself with rigorous care and exhausting studies for the rest of your suffering and uncertain life; renounce the attractions of love, the intoxications of pleasure, the sweet repose of the spring nights; and, on the day when you think you have deserved a crown, they will load you with irons, they will cover you with shame; and the blind and fickle public, which finds it so hard to welcome the truth, always receives calumny with open arms! Be sure of it, Valerio, this very moment these people who have seen me since the day of my birth growing up and living in the love of my work, hating injustice and respecting the laws, these people who judge human consciences only by the reverses or successes of fortune, — be sure of it, they accuse me already, although it is only ten minutes since they knew of my being in prison. That I am unfortunate is enough to make them believe that I am culpable. They no longer make any distinction between my name and that of Vincent Bianchini. Both of us have been accused, both of us have known the disgrace of imprisonment. I may be set free; perhaps I am innocent. But did they never set free one who was guilty? Who knows if, like him, I shall not be banished? Does not Venice banish all whom she distrusts? and does she not distrust all who are denounced to her?"

Valerio realized that his brother's suffering was only too well founded, and that in trying to reconcile him to his situation he only made him feel more keenly the severity and danger of it. Towards evening he was preparing to go out to procure some food for him and a cloak; but when he called the jailer, through the slide in the door, he was informed that orders had been received not to allow him to go out again, and the jailer even showed him a paper, bearing the seal of the Inquisitors of the State, which ordered the arrest of the two brothers Zuccati, without expressing upon what ground of provocation. Francesco uttered a cry of anguish upon hearing of this arrest.

"They will kill me," said he. "The butchers! could they not make an end of me without torturing me with the sight of my brother's suffering?"

"Do not pity me," answered Valerio. "They might not have allowed me to spend the days and nights with you. Now I thank them, and I shall never leave you."

Many days and many nights passed by, yet the Zuccati brothers received no light as to their position, no relief from their sadness and anxiety. The heat was oppressive; the plague had broken out in Venice, and the air of the prison was infectious. Francesco, lying on his bed of rough and dusty straw, no longer seemed to realize his misfortune; from time to time he reached out his arm to convey to his lips some drops of brackish water in a pewter mug. Exhausted by continual sweats, he wiped his smarting face with the linen rags which Valerio kept for him with extreme care, and took the trouble to wash each day, setting aside for this purpose half his miserable allowance of water. It was almost the only service he could render his unfortunate brother. Everything was wanting. He had used all his rich clothing to make, with the aid of some straw, a kind of pillow and a parasol for him. He had kept for himself only a few tatters upon which there still shone some remnants of gold and of embroidery. He had tried in vain to offer his pearls, his poniard, and his golden chain to the jailers in order to procure for Francesco some relief from the frightful regimen of the hard prison fare. The jailors of the Inquisition were not to be bribed.

In spite of the impossibility of helping his brother in his present situation, Valerio remained constantly near him. Stronger than Francesco, and too much absorbed in his suffering to feel his own, he busied himself turning him on his miserable bed, fanning him with the great plume of his cap, feeling his burning hands, and watching his languid eyes. Francesco no longer complained. He had lost his hope. Whenever for a moment he roused from his lethargy, he made an effort to smile upon his brother, spoke a few tender words to him, and immediately fell back into a dreadful stupor.

One evening Valerio was seated as usual upon the

scorching brick floor. Francesco's heavy head was resting on his knee. The pitiless sun was setting in a sea of fire, and cast a sinister reflection upon the red walls, which seemed mercilessly to absorb and retain its intense heat. The plague was spreading farther and farther. All the exhilarating, gladsome sounds of brilliant Venice had given place to the silence of death, broken only by the mournful tolling of the bell for the dying, and by the distant chant of some pious monk passing along the canal, conveying to the cemetery a boat filled with dead bodies. A martin lighted on the chink in the roof which admitted an occasional whiff of dry air into the lodging of the Zuccati. This black swallow, with his breast the color of blood, his note loud and piercing, and his proud, untamed aspect, had the effect of a bad omen on Valerio. It seemed restless; and, after having called, as is its custom, to bring back some belated comrade, it flew up through the air uttering a certain cry which the Venetians knew well, and which they never heard without a kind of terror. It is the cry which calls these wandering birds together when the time has come for them to change their hemisphere. They go away together in numerous bands. The sky is obscured by them, and the same day sees them all disappear, even to the last one. Their departure is the signal for a veritable scourge. The *mozelins*, those imperceptible insects, whose thin and continual humming irritates even to the point of fever, and whose bite is unendurable, fill the atmosphere, and, being no longer driven to the higher regions of the air by the hunting swallows, they swarm about the dwellings, infest them, and steal the sleep from all Venetians, whom wealth, with all its resources, does not preserve from their attacks.

In prison, and at a time when the air, filled with pestilential exhalations, entered with venomous stings into all the pores, the arrival of the *mozelins*, soon to be followed by that of scorpions, was a death signal for Francesco. Already consumed with a violent fever, he managed to enjoy a little rest for a few short hours in the night when the refreshing breeze reached him. But this rest was to be taken from him. It was during the night that little gnats penetrated into all the dwellings, especially into those where the heated breath of man attracted them. Valerio listened anxiously. He heard a thousand piercing cries, a thousand restless, hurried chatterings, a calling and answering, a flying away and returning, a uniting again and collecting on the roofs as if to deliberate, then a darting away with a piercing farewell cry, like a last malediction upon the sorrowing city. Valerio placed himself in the dormer window, where he could see nothing but the sky. He saw the black specks moving in the heavens at an immeasurable height, no longer describing the great regular circles of the chase, but flying in a straight line direct for the east. It was the martins already on their way. Francesco had heard their parting cry; he had read on Valerio's face the fearful effect of this discovery. When suffering overpowers man, he cannot conceive of an increase of suffering, however imminent and unavoidable; he has not the strength to add, even in thought, future evil to present evil. When this evil comes, he is as if crushed under an unforeseen catastrophe. Death itself, that final thing, so fatal, so inevitable, surprises almost all men as if it were an injustice from Heaven, a freak of destiny.

"Counting from to-morrow," said Francesco to his brother in a faint voice, "I shall sleep no more." He pronounced his own death sentence. Valerio understood it, and let his head fall upon his breast. The scalding tears, which until then he had had the stoicism to repress, rolled in floods down his pale and emaciated cheeks.

XVI.

THE Inquisition was a power so mysterious, so absolute, there was so much danger involved in trying to penetrate its secrets, and this was so difficult to do, that three days after Saint Mark's nobody spoke any more of the Zuccati. The report of Francesco's arrest had spread rapidly, and this report had died away like the wave which breaks on the silent and desert shore. The slightest rock would repulse and excite it; but a sandy shore, for a long time smoothed and devastated by the storms, receives the surges without resistance, and all their force is annihilated for want of provocation: such was Venice. The restless effervescence, the natural curiosity of her people, spent themselves like the empty foam of the waves on the shores of the ducal palace, and the dark waters which bathed its quays bore at every hour a stream of blood, the unknown source of which was hidden in the bowels of this mysterious den.

Moreover, the plague had come, filling all hearts with alarm and discouragement. All work was suspended, all the schools were dispersed. Marini had been attacked among the first, and was struggling with a slow and painful convalescence. Ceccato had lost one of his children, and was devoting himself to his death-stricken wife. The anger of the Bianchini had been stifled momentarily by the fear of death. Bozza had disappeared.

Old Sebastian Zuccato had retired to the country on the Feast of Saint Mark, at the breaking up of the games, in a bad humor at what he called the extravagance and vainglory of his sons. He was wholly ignorant of their misfortune, and fretted at not seeing them, as usual, pacifying his anger by their respectful attentions.

The plague having lost a little of its malignity, old Zuccato was afraid at last that his sons might have succumbed to it. He came to Venice, determined to be severe with them, but full of anxiety; and the more irritated he was against them, the more he felt how impossible it was not to love them. It must not be thought that, after the scene at the basilica, Sebastian was reconciled to mosaic work. He was always prejudiced against it, and against those who gave themselves to it. If he had, in spite of himself, yielded to the power which great things exercise over artists' souls, if he did press his children to his heart and shower upon them tears of tenderness, he had not, for all that, abandoned any of his preconceived ideas regarding the superiority of certain branches of art. Even had he wished it, he was not the master to give up at the hour of death the ideas he had obstinately cherished all his life. The only thing which consoled him was the hope that Francesco would some day renounce this vile metal work, and return to his easel. With the intention of exhorting him anew, he went to the basilica, thinking to find him busy on some other cupola. But he found the basilica draped in black, and heard mournful chants resounding through the gloomy arches. The wax tapers, struggling with the last rays of day, diffused a dull red glimmer, more appalling than the darkness. The last honors were being paid to two Senators who had died of the plague. Their catafalques were under the portico. All was done hastily, and it was easy to see that the priests fulfilled their sacred duties with fear and precipitation. The old Zuccato trembled from head to foot on seeing these two caskets. He could only reassure himself by learning the names of these two dead magistrates. Then he left the church, and ran to Valerio's studio in San Filippo. But there he was told that neither Francesco nor Valerio had been seen since Saint Mark's Day; and he sought with no better success in all the places where they were in the habit of going. Finally, when beside himself with anxiety, he succeeded in finding poor Ceccato, and inferred from his gloomy forebodings that his sons must be dead in prison either through grief or sickness. He remained for some moments immovable, absorbed, and pale as death. At last he departed, and, without a word to Ceccato or his disconsolate family, he went to the abode of the *Procurator-Cassiere*. He was far from accusing this magistrate of the unjust arrest of his sons. Naturally patient, he would have thought himself wanting in respect and love for the laws in suspecting a magistrate guilty of error or prejudice. Dissatisfied with his sons, and ready to accuse them of idleness or insolence according to the decision of the Procurator, at least he wished to know at any cost what had become of them. So he humbly approached the great *Cassiere*, who, doubtless to preserve himself from the plague, was more than ever occupied with his own well-being. He found him surrounded by flagons and aromatics of all kinds to purify the air which he breathed. Nevertheless, Sebastian's ceremonious salutations made him a little more tractable than he was ordinarily.

"That 'll do, that 'll do," said he, making a sign to Sebastian to keep at a distance, and enveloping his nose in a large handkerchief saturated with essence of juniper. "Far enough, my man. Don't come so near, and hold your breath a little. By the cap! in these cursed times we do not know to whom we are speaking. Are n't you sick? Come, hurry up! What is the matter?"

"Your respected Lordship," answered the old man, slightly mortified at this unceremonious welcome, "sees before you the syndic of painters, Sebastian Zuccato, your very humble servant, and the father of —"

"Ah! so," replied Melchior, without disturbing himself save by a feint of touching languidly his black silk cap, which fitted close to his flat head. "I did not remember you, Messer Zuccato. You are an honest man, but your sons are two cunning knaves."

"Your Excellency, the word is a little severe. I cannot deny that my sons may be bad enough subjects, very dissipated, very obstinate in their ideas, and devoted to a very foolish and very contemptible calling. I know they have incurred the displeasure of our lords, the magistrates, and yours in particular. I am sure they must have committed some grave fault, since your kindness to them has changed to severity. I do not come to justify them, but to appease your anger, and to beg that your mercy will take into consideration the poisonous air, the severity of the season, and the delicate health of my eldest son, which has been sufficiently endangered by prison fare for him to remember this punishment and not expose himself to it again."

"Your son is indeed sick, they tell me," replied the Procurator. "But who is not sick during this malignant time? I am suffering a great deal myself, and without the assiduous care of my physician I should have died, I do not doubt. But one must take precautions, great precautions. By the ducal cap! I advise you also, Master Sebastian, to take precautions."

"Your Excellency says that my son Francesco is sick?" said Sebastian, affrighted.

"Oh, that need not disturb you: one is no worse off in prison than anywhere else. We know by exact statistics that the death rate among prisoners under the leads is no greater than in other prisons of the Republic."

"Under the leads,[1] your Excellency!" cried old Zuccato. "Your Lordship said under the leads! Are my sons under the leads?"

"By the cap! they are, and they deserve no less for their extortions and sponging."

"My God! Monsignore, you wish to frighten me," said Zuccato in a loud voice, and recoiling a step. "My children are not under the leads!"

"They are, I tell you," answered the Procurator; "and I cannot take them out until their process is prepared and judged. As soon as the plague will permit us to attend to their case, we shall do so; but, by the ducal cap! I am much afraid their coming out will be only for the worse, for they are guilty, and perpetual banishment is the penalty for those who steal the public funds."

"By the body of the devil! Messer," cried the old man, drawing near to the Procurator, "whoever says that lies in his throat, and those who have put my sons under the leads will repent of it while I can raise a finger."

"Do not come near me," cried Melchior in his turn, rising quickly and pushing back his arm-chair. "Do not let me feel your breath on my face. If

[1] The prison in the upper story of the ducal palace, which has a leaden roof.

you've got the plague, keep it, and go to the devil with your rascally sons. I tell you they will be hanged if you aggravate their case by making a noise. All the Zuccati are villanous knaves. Upon my word, you poison the air, Messer. Get out!"

While uttering these words, Melchior continually drew back, and the old Zuccato, motionless in his place, gave him a look that froze him with terror.

"If I had the plague," said he at last, in a sepulchral voice, "I should like to fold in my arms all those who dare to say that the Zuccati are robbers. I hope this idea has never come to any one, and that the magistrate to whom I have the honor of speaking may be seized with fever and delirium this very moment. Yes, yes, Monsignore, it is the pestilence speaking through you when you say that the Zuccati have kept the public money. Know that the Zuccati come of noble race, and that the blood which courses through their veins is purer than that of the ducal families. Know that Francesco and Valerio are two men whom they may indeed put to death by torture, but whom they cannot dishonor. Your Lordship will do well to call your physician, for a mortal venom is running through your veins."

Finishing these terrible words, Sebastian darted out of the *Procuraties*, and ran to the ducal palace.

Melchior rang his bell in great agitation, called for his doctor, and made him bleed, rub, and physic him all night, believing that old Zuccato had given him the plague by witchcraft. He fainted away many times, and nearly died with fear.

XVII.

SEBASTIAN ZUCCATO hastened to throw himself at the feet of the Doge, and demanded justice with all the eloquence of paternal love and outraged honor. Mocenigo listened to him kindly, and showed him marks of the highest esteem. He regretted much the prolonged torture to which his sons had been subjected, and took it upon himself to have them transferred to less grewsome quarters. He even allowed the old Sebastian to see them every day, and to administer to them such care as his tenderness suggested. But he did not conceal from him that the most serious charges had been preferred against them, and that their case would be a long and weighty affair.

However, thanks to his persistent importunity, old Zuccato, with the influence of Titian, Tintoretto, and many other great masters, all friends of the Zuccati, thanks also to the kind protection of the Doge, the Council of Ten, whose functions had been suspended for several months owing to the epidemic, assembled at last; and the first question this august tribunal attacked was the case against the Zuccati, accused: —

"1. Of having stolen their salary, because their work was hastily done and without solidity; for instance, by working out of season (*fuor di stagione*), that is to say, in cold weather, when work in mastic does not hold, in order to make up for the time they had lost during the fine season in promenades, dissipations, and debaucheries of all kinds;

"2. Of having made figures badly drawn and grotesquely colored, the result of obstinately working the greater part of the night to make up for their previous laziness (*ingordigia*);

"3. Of having done this detestable work through their entire ignorance of their business, an ignorance which rendered Valerio Zuccato incapable of accomplishing anything but senseless articles for the toilets of women and young people (*culfie, fraslagli, vesture*, etc.), which childish performance occupied him incessantly, and afforded him a lucrative profession at San Filippo, while the public paid him handsomely for work which he did not and could not do;

"4. Of having, by contemptible trickery, used in many places painted pieces of wood and pasteboard instead of enamel and stone (*i pezzi*) in order to show a degree of detail of which the mosaic materials are not susceptible, thereby acquiring for themselves the credit of great artistic merit during their lives, only to leave behind them works which would last no longer."

The documents relating to this strange case are still to be found in the archives of the ducal palace; and Signor Quadri has given a faithful account of it, which can be read in an article entitled "Dei Musaici," at the end of his excellent work on Venetian painting.

The plaintiffs were the *Procurator-Cassiere* Melchior, Bartolommeo Bozza, the three Bianchini, Jean Viscentin, and several other pupils of their school, and finally Claude de Corrége, organist of St. Mark's, who hated the noise of the workmen, and who would have testified equally in favor of the Zuccati and against the Bianchini, hoping that, wearied with these quarrels and useless expenses, the government would give up these extravagant repairs, the principal inconvenience of which, in the eyes of the organist, was the annoyance this continual racket occasioned to his school of plain chant held in the organ loft.

The witnesses in favor of the Zuccati were Titian and his son Orazio, Tintoretto, Paolo Veronese,

Marini, Ceccato, and the good priest Alberto Zio. All of them appeared before the Council of Ten, and vouched for the great talent, beautiful work, proper behavior, close application, and perfect honesty of the Zuccati brothers and all their school.

In their turn the Zuccati brothers were brought before the judges. Valerio supported his dear brother in his arms, scarcely recovered from his long and serious illness, faint, crushed, apparently indifferent to the issue of the trial which he no longer had the strength to bear. Valerio was pale and thin. He had been provided with clothing; but his long beard, his hair carelessly combed, his halting step, and a certain convulsive trembling, testified to his suffering and his grief. Indifferent to his own wrongs, but indignant at the injustice done his brother, life, at last, had become a serious matter to him. Anger and revenge flashed in his eyes; a dull fire shot from them, now sunken with famine, fatigue, and mental agony. In passing before Bartolommeo Bozza to take his place upon the bench for the accused, he raised his two arms laden with chains as if he would crush him, and his face, blazing with rage, said, "I would like to send you under the earth."

The guards restrained him, and he sat down, still

holding Francesco's cold, trembling hand in his own.

"Francesco Zuccato," said the judge, "you are accused of theft and fraud against the Republic; what have you to say?"

"I say," answered Francesco, "that I might as well be accused of murder and parricide, if it be the good pleasure of those who persecute me."

"And I," said Valerio, impetuously, rising to his feet, "I say that we lie under an outrageous accusation, and that for three months we have suffered in prison, from which my brother has come out in a dying condition, and all because the Bianchini hate us, and because Bozza, our pupil, is a scoundrel; but particularly because the Procurator, Monsignore Melchior, made a mistake in Latin, which we took upon ourselves to correct. It is the first time two citizens were ever imprisoned for not wishing to commit a barbarism."

Valerio's wrath was not calculated to win the good will of the magistrate. The old Zuccato, seeing the unfortunate effect of this harangue, arose and said:—

"Silence, my son. You talk like an impudent fool. This is not the way in which an honest citizen should defend himself before the fathers of his country.

Gentlemen, excuse his rudeness. These poor young men are suffering from fever. Examine their case according to your unswerving equity. If they are guilty, punish them without pity: their father will be the first to praise you for this act of justice, and to bless the severity of the laws which chastise fraud. Yes, yes, were it necessary to shed their blood myself, I would do it, my fathers, before I would see the august power of the Republic fall into discredit. But if they are innocent, as I am convinced they are, make them prompt and generous redress; for you see my eldest son here has no longer but a breath of life left in him; and as for the younger, you see he is delirious."

Saying this with a strong voice, the old man fell on his knees, while tears rolled copiously down his long white beard.

"Sebastian Zuccato," answered the judge, "the Republic knows your veracity and your loyalty. You have spoken as becomes a good father and a good citizen, but if you have nothing else to say in defence of your sons you must withdraw."

At a sign from the magistrate, the vassal who had led in Sebastian, led him away. The old man cast a look of despair upon his two sons as he passed out, and, joining his hands, raised his eyes to heaven with an expression so heart-rending it might have melted the marble pillars of the great hall; but the Council of Ten was colder and more inflexible than they.

After the three Bianchini had affirmed their accusation upon oath, Bartolommeo Bozza, being summoned in his turn to the witness stand, placed his hand upon the crucifix which was presented to him, and said:—

"I swear upon the Christ that I have passed three months under the leads for not being willing to bear false witness."

A movement of surprise passed over the assembly. Melchior knit his brows. Bianchini the Red ground his teeth, and young Valerio, rising impatiently, exclaimed,—

"Is it true? O my poor pupil! And can I still pity and love you? Ah! this thought sweetens all my pain."

"Silence, Valerio Zuccato," said the judge, "and let the witness speak."

Bartolommeo was as weak and sick as the Zuccati. He also had been subjected to the slow torture of imprisonment. He testified that, some days before the Feast of Saint Mark, Vincent Bianchini had conducted him to the scaffolding of the Zuccati that he might see close to and touch many places in their work where painted pasteboard had evidently been used instead of stone, and that from there he had taken him to the house of the *Procurator-Cassiere* to make affidavit to that effect, which he did in the indignation and sincerity of his heart. From that day, being convinced of the trickery practised by the Zuccati, and not wishing to be an accomplice in a work which could not fail to be condemned, he had worked in the school of the Bianchini. But Vincent on the eve of Saint Mark's, having again conducted him to the Procurator, had wished to make him promise to testify that he had been an eyewitness of the facts as set forth in the accusation: this he had refused to do, because, if he had seen the proofs of the fraud, at least he had not seen the fraud committed. "If I had seen it," said he, "I should not have waited for an invitation from the Bianchini before leaving the school of the Zuccati. But I had never seen anything of the kind. There was not the slightest thing in the behavior of my masters up to that time to give a show of truth to the discovery which was brought under my observation. It was therefore impossible for me to swear by the Christ that I had seen them use cardboard and paint. When Vincent Bianchini saw that I did not serve his purpose as he wished, he turned against me and accused me of duplicity with the Zuccati. Monsignore Melchior made me a great many threats, which provoked me to such a degree that I told him to beware of the Bianchini. That same evening I was arrested and imprisoned. From that day I have believed that my old masters were innocent, and that the man capable of asking me to take a false oath was also capable, unknown to the Zuccati and all the world, of having destroyed a part of the mosaic work during the night, and of having replaced the stone by wood and pasteboard, for the purpose of ruining them. I should state that this substitution is effected with so much skill that without scratching these pieces (*i pezzi*) a little it is impossible to detect it."

Thus spoke Bozza with a firm voice, and a Bolognese accent very slow and distinct. Summoned to express his opinion upon the continual diversions to which Valerio devoted himself, he admitted that this young master had often been reprimanded for idleness and dissipation by his elder brother, and that he made up afterwards for lost time by working nights, which might justify the reproach conveyed in the accusation of his having made works without solidity (*fuor di stagione*). He also stated that Valerio did not understand metal work as well as his brother, and that he made many ornamental objects according to his own particular fancy. In a word, it was easy to see that he was not speaking out of any kind feeling for the Zuccati, and that he would not have been in the least sorry had he hurt them by telling the truth. But he had a horror of the lie in which the Bianchini had wished to entrap him, and whom he would never forgive for having caused his imprisonment.

The Council closed the day's session by nominating a committee of painters authorized to examine, under the eyes of the Procurators, the work of the two rival schools. The committee was composed of Titian, Tintoretto, Paolo Veronese, Jacopo Pistoja, and Andrea Schiavone, who from that time was called *Medola*, owing to the pains he took to analyze mosaic work to the utmost.

XVIII.

THE following day, these illustrious masters, accompanied by their workmen, the Procurators, and some of the officers of the Inquisition, went to St. Mark's, and proceeded to the examination of the mosaic works. At the request of the Bianchini, they began with the genealogical tree of the Virgin, an immense work completed in a very short time. Vincent, in addition to all his vices, was possessed of an insurmountable pride. Eager for praise, he followed Titian step by step, always anticipating an outburst of admiration. Beside him walked Dominique the Red, his eyes glistening with a settled, idiotic confidence. But Titian did not express his opinion. Always considerate and courteous, he continued to address to them words which showed attention and interest, but which in no way compromised his judgment as a connoisseur. His polished manners, his gracious smiles, contrasted with Tintoretto's darkening brow and austere countenance. Although perhaps less intimate with the

Zuccati, Robusti was much more indignant than Titian at the wickedness of their rivals. In Titian's soul, accustomed as he was himself to feelings of deep hatred and implacable animosity, the conduct of the Bianchini found, if not an excuse, at least a more indulgent comprehension of the jealousy of the workman and the ambition of the artist. Perhaps also Tintoretto, recalling the trials to which he had been obliged to submit on the part of Titian, took advantage of the moment to give him a just rebuke by showing his own horror and contempt for this sort of thing. He left the chapel of St. Isidore without opening his lips, and without once turning his eyes towards those who accompanied him.

But when he was under the great dome, and had before his eyes the works of the Zuccati, he broke forth into expressions of eloquent praise. His beautiful austere head was animated with the fire of enthusiasm, and he enlarged upon all the perfections of this work with generous warmth. Titian, who was the intimate friend of old Sebastian, and who had given many valuable lessons to the young Zuccati, surpassed him in his praise, without, however, depreciating the work of the Bianchini, before whom he was very cautious. But the *Procurator-*

Cassiere, annoyed at the success of the Zuccati, took up the word.

"Gentlemen," said he to the illustrious masters, "I must remind you that we have not come here to look at paintings, but at mosaic work. It matters very little to the State whether the hand of the Virgin be modelled more or less according to the rules of your art. It matters still less whether in the leg of Saint Isidore the calf be a little too high or a little too low. All this is very well as a subject for discussion—"

"How!" cried Titian, who at this impious speech forgot for the moment his guarded courtesy,—"it matters little to the State that mosaic-workers do not understand drawing, and that the mosaics are not elegant and correct reproductions of the works of the painters? This is the first time that I have heard of such a thing, Monsignore, and it will require all the respect with which your judgment inspires me to make me embrace this opinion."

Nothing heightened the erroneous convictions of the *Procurator-Cassiere* like contradiction.

"And I, Messer Tiziano," he exclaimed with heat, "I assure you that all that is insignificant and childish. These are quarrels of the school and discussions of the studio, in which the dignity of the magistracy will not allow itself to be compromised. Commissioned by the Republic to watch over its interests, and to conduct the public expenses honestly and economically, the Procurators will not permit the works of St. Mark's to fall short of their contract for the useless pleasure of amusing amateurs in painting."

"I did not think," said Francesco Zuccato in a feeble voice, and casting a pitiful look upon his work, "that I could fall short of my contract by following as closely as possible the models of my figures, and in conforming conscientiously to all the rules of my art."

"I know the rules of your art as well as you, Messer," said the Procurator, red with anger; "you cannot make me believe that a mosaic-worker must of necessity be a painter. The Republic pays you for servilely and faithfully reproducing the cartoons of the painters, and provided you fasten your stones solidly and neatly to the wall, provided you know how to use good materials and to adapt them to the purposes for which they are intended, it matters very little that you should know the rules of painting and drawing. By the ducal cap! if you were such great artists, the Republic could be very economical. It would no longer have to pay Messer

Vecelli and Messer Robusti for designing your models. You could be allowed to compose, direct, and draw your own subjects. Unfortunately, we have not enough confidence in you as master painters to trust them to you."

"Nevertheless, Monsignore," said Titian, who had recovered his calm and who knew how to give a benign expression to the contemptuous smile playing about his lips, "I venture to object to your Lordship, that, in order to know how to copy a good drawing faithfully, one must himself be a good artist. Were it not so, one might trust Raphael's cartoons to the first schoolboy that presented himself, and it would suffice that one have a grand model under his eyes to constitute him at once a great artist. Things are not done in this way, as your Lordship will permit me to say, with all the respect which I profess for your opinions; but it is one thing to govern men by sublime wisdom, and another to amuse them with frivolous talents. We should be very much perplexed, we poor artisans, if, like your Lordship, we had to hold the reins of the State with a firm and generous hand; but—"

"But you pretend, flatterer," said the Procurator, somewhat softened, "that you understand what pertains to painting and mosaic work better than we. You will not deny, at least, that solidity is one of the indispensable conditions of this kind of work, and if, instead of using stone, crystal, marble, and enamel, one employs pasteboard, wood, oil, and varnish, you will admit that the funds of the Republic have not been put to their proper use."

Here Titian was slightly embarrassed, for he did not know how much foundation there might be for this accusation of the Bianchini, and he feared to compromise the Zuccati by any imprudent remark.

"I deny, at least," said he, after a moment's pause, "that this substitution of material constitutes a fraud, provided it be proved, as I think it can be, that the brush may be used in certain places of mosaic work with as much solidity as enamel."

"Very well, this is what we are going to find out, Messer Vecelli," said the Procurator, "for we do not wish to doubt your sincerity in this matter. Let us have some sand and a sponge here; and by the cap! we'll have it rubbed thick all over these walls."

Francesco's lifeless eyes glistened, and turned with comtemptible hatred toward the inscription where the word *Saxis* had replaced the barbarism *Saxibus*. He thought to himself, if he should be condemned for the substitution of a single letter, he would console himself for it by seeing the blunder of the

Procurator made public. Melchior understood his thought, and read his look; he avoided applying the test here, and carried it to other parts of the dome.

The mosaics of the Zuccati, thoroughly rubbed and washed in all places, withstood the experiment perfectly; no part of it fell nor was likely to fall. The *Procurator-Cassiere* began to think that the avowed hatred of the Bianchini and his own prejudice had misled him in an affair but little to his credit, when Vincent Bianchini, approaching the two archangels, one of which was the portrait of Valerio and the other of Francesco Zuccati, said boldly: —

"It is true that wood and painted pasteboard may resist sand and a wet sponge, but it is not true that they can resist the influence of time, and here is a proof of it." So saying, he took out his stiletto, and, punching it into the naked breast of the archangel which represented Francesco Zuccato near to the heart, he started a piece of flesh-colored substance, which he quickly cut in two with his knife and handed to the Procurators. The fragment being passed from hand to hand, Titian himself was forced to admit that it was a piece of wood.

XIX.

FRANCESCO and Valerio were led back to prison, and eight days afterwards they appeared again before the Council of Ten. The *procès-verbal* report, drawn up by the commission of painters, was read aloud to them. They avoided any allusion to the inferiority of the works of the Bianchini. They knew that to depreciate them as works of art would irritate the *Procurator-Cassiere* more and more, and, the affairs of the Zuccati having taken a sufficiently bad turn, prudence required that they should not further excite their enemies; but they were profuse in their praise of the cupola of the Zuccati, and they had proved the solidity of all this work with the exception of two unimportant figures, where wood had been used instead of stone. Titian had even affirmed that he thought this painted mosaic work capable of resisting the ravages of time for five hundred years or more; and his prediction is verified, for these pieces spoken of in the process are still in existence, and apparently as beautiful and solid as the other parts of the mosaic work. As to the ability of the young Zuccato, charged by his accusers of incapacity or ignorance, he was gloriously vindicated by the *procès-verbal*, and declared at least as capable as his brother.

After this statement, the whole accusation rested only upon one point, that of the substitution of unusual material in the execution of the figures of the two archangels.

Francesco, questioned as to what he had to offer in his defence, said that, having been for a long time convinced of the advantage of this substitution for certain details, and anxious to prove its solidity, he had ventured to try it in these two figures, which were of little importance, and which he always meant to repair at his own expense if its durability did not fulfil his expectations, or if the Republic was opposed to such an innovation.

The Council did not seem willing to accept this excuse. Pressed by accusations and threats, Valerio could not control his temper.

"Very well," said he, "since you wish to know, learn the secret that my brother wished to keep. In telling it to you, I know very well that I expose myself, not only to the hatred and envy which are already brought to bear against us, but also to that

THE MASTER MOSAIC-WORKERS.

of all our future rivals. I know that rude workmen and vile mechanics will be indignant at seeing in us conscientious artists. I know they will pretend to consider mosaic work nothing but a work of simple masonry, and that they will persecute as unworthy companions and ambitious rivals any one who tries to make an art of it, and bring to it the fire of enthusiasm or the light of intelligence. Very well, I object to such blasphemy. I say that a true mosaic-worker ought to be an artist, and I assert that my brother Francesco, the pupil of his father and of Messer Tiziano, is a great painter; and I prove it by declaring that the two figures of the archangels which have obtained the praise of the illustrious commission nominated by the Council, were conceived, composed, designed, and colored by my brother, whose apprentice I was, and the workman who faithfully copied his cartoons. Perhaps we have been guilty of a serious crime for taking upon ourselves to consecrate our best work to the Republic, offering it gratis and privately, with a modesty becoming young men and with a prudence becoming young men who acknowledge another God than money and public favor; but when we are accused of fraud, we are forced to set aside this prudence and modesty. We ask, therefore, that it be proved whether we have tried this innovation except in a composition not required of us, and which we are ready to remove from the basilica if the government considers it unworthy to appear beside the works of the Bianchini."

Upon examining the cartoons of the various compositions designed by the painters and intrusted to the mosaic-workers, they did not find these two archangel figures. The Procurator Melchior urged each of the painters to give his opinion upon the merits of these figures, and to specify what they had had to do with them. As they had been invested by the State with all rights and all power in regard to these things, a simple sketch drawn by one of them would have sufficed to prove that the Zuccati, bound to execute to the letter their designs, had rendered themselves guilty of unfaithfulness, disobedience, and fraud in executing them according to a method of their own, and in using material not approved by the Commission of Procurators. The painters declared upon oath that they had not had even an idea of these figures; and as to their merit they also stated that they themselves would not have been able to create anything more correct or more noble. Titian was questioned twice. They knew his friendship for the Zuccati; they knew also his tact, his

THE MASTER MOSAIC-WORKERS.

ingenuity in evading the questions he did not wish to answer. Summoned to say whether he was the author of these figures, he answered courteously, "I wish I were, but, to tell the truth, I have not even seen the design of them, and I had no suspicion of their existence until, as a member of the commission, I was ordered to examine them."

The Bianchini maintained that the Zuccati were not capable of designing works worthy of so much praise without assistance. In spite of the declarations of the painters, they held an inquiry to which Bozza was summoned, and, as an old pupil of the Zuccati, he was requested to state if he had seen any painter touch these figures. He replied, that once only he had seen Messer Orazio Vecelli, Titian's son, come by night to the studio of the Zuccati at the time when they were working there. Orazio was summoned, and declared upon oath that he had not even seen them, and that his visit to the studio of San Filippo by night was for no other object than to order from Valerio a mosaic bracelet which he wished to present to a lady. There was no longer any proof against the Zuccati. They were acquitted, on the sole condition of replacing at their own expense, by pieces of stone and enamel, the fragments of painted wood employed in certain details of their

THE MASTER MOSAIC-WORKERS.

figures. This part of the decree was simply a matter of form, in order not to encourage innovators. They did not even insist on the execution of it, for the painted pieces are there still. The barbarism of the *Procurator-Cassiere* alone has been restored according to the manner in which it came forth from the learned brain of this magistrate, and above the two archangels we read this other touching inscription, alluding to the persecutions suffered by the Zuccati: —

UBI DILIGENTER INSPEXERIS ARTEMQ. AC LABOREM FRANCISCI ET VALERII ZVCATI VENETORVM FRATRVM AGNOVERIS TVM DEMVM IVDICATO.

XX.

IN spite of the fortunate termination of this legal process, much was required before the fortunes of the Zuccati took on a happy aspect. Francesco's health returned slowly. No new public work was demanded of the mosaic-workers. There was some talk even of keeping them at a standstill, and of preserving all the old Byzantine works, for fashion had taken an austere turn, and while the wise sumptuary laws covered the cloaks and gondolas with mourning, the people, less serious, through a spirit of imitation, wrapped themselves in long Roman togas, and wore ornaments of iron and silver only. The word "economy" was on every lip. The plague had paralyzed commerce, and, as generations pass readily from one excess to another, after ruinous luxury and foolish expenditures came a time of penurious retrenchments and childish reforms. Artists fared ill in these hours of financial depression. The *Procurator-Cassiere* was not an isolated fool, but the representative of a great number of narrow souls.

Francesco had fallen into a state of deep despondency. An enthusiastic artist, he had aspired to and hoped for glory. He had served her as one serves a noble mistress, by noble sacrifices, with an ardent and exclusive worship. For his sole recompense, he had seen himself exposed to an infamous imprisonment, imminent death, and a disgraceful lawsuit. Moreover, the success of his masterpieces was questioned. Men do not see without chastisement misfortune burst upon the head of the elect. They are seized, therefore, with a vertigo of mediocrity, and try in all manner of ways to excuse and justify the evils with which genius is stricken. It was enough to have found a small piece of wood in one of the little figures of the Zuccati for the public to conclude at once that the whole mosaic work was executed in wood. The illiterate even went so far as to say it was of paper, and, convinced of its want of solidity, they would have considered it a lack of patriotism to lift their heads in order to admire the beauty of the figures. The young artist was wounded to the depths of his soul, and suffered the more as he carefully concealed his wound, and hated the public too much to give it the satisfaction of seeing him vanquished. Closely shut up in his little room at San Filippo, he passed his days at the window absorbed in sad thoughts, and was only distracted from his misery by watching the great ivies of the court swaying in the breeze. This quiet scene was refreshing to him after his sojourn under the leads, where the want of air had slowly undermined his life.

During the time of his success and his sumptuous amusements, Valerio had fallen considerably into debt. His creditors tormented him. Francesco found out this secret, and devoted all his savings to the payment of these debts. Valerio knew this only a long time afterward. He was sad enough without remorse being added to the anxiety caused him by his dear brother's health. The thought of losing him shook his very soul, and he felt that, in spite of his natural disposition to accept the ills of life, he could never console himself for his loss. Incapable of melancholy, too strong for resignation and too strong also for despair, he often fell into violent states of indignation, followed by brilliant hopes, and he entertained Francesco with dreams of fame and happiness, although really at heart no one needed glory less than he in order to be happy.

Old Sebastian begged them to return to the brush,

and give up this vile mosaic work. But Francesco had received too rude a shock to yield himself to fresh hopes. To undertake a new career at thirty required a resolution beyond the power of a spirit so wounded, a body so weakened. To his suffering was added that of his friends. His disgrace had caused Ceccato to lose his prerogatives as master; both he and Marini were in a state of absolute want. In vain Francesco solicited the payment for his year's work. The finances, like all other departments of the administration, were dull and in disorder. All his efforts were useless. They put him off from day to day, from week to week. The secret hatred of the *Procurator-Cassiere* had something to do with these postponements of payment. By this subtle vengeance he paid back the irony of the Zuccati, too little punished in his opinion by the Council.

The Zuccati were resolved to share their last crust of bread with their faithful apprentices. They fed Marini, Ceccato, his young convalescent wife, and his remaining child. Valerio still obtained some money from the Greeks stationed in Venice, by selling them jewelry; but this resource would not be sufficient for such a numerous family after Francesco's savings should be spent. Then Valerio reproached himself bitterly for not having laid by anything; he realized too late that prodigality is a vice. "Yes, yes," said he with a sigh, "the man who spends what he earns by the sweat of his brow in empty amusement and foolish display does not deserve to have friends, because he cannot aid them in the day of distress."

So it was necessary for him to see by what indefatigable zeal and skilful application he could repair the faults of the past. He had divided his narrow room into three compartments,—a studio, a refectory, and a sleeping-room for Francesco. At night he slept on a mat in the first convenient corner, oftener on the terrace raised above the roof. During the day he worked assiduously, and got his apprentices to make mosaic pictures, hoping always that the time would come when works of art would no longer be ranked as luxuries and objects of fancy. He alone attended to all the details of the housekeeping, and, if he allowed Ceccato's wife to prepare the dinner, he did not permit her to fatigue herself in the least by going to purchase it. He went himself to the fish market, to the vegetable market, to the *frittole*, and he might be seen, covered with perspiration, threading the winding streets with a basket under his cloak. If he met any of the young noblemen who heretofore had shared his pleasures and his generosity, he carefully evaded them, or obstinately concealed his poverty from them, fearing they might send assistance to him, the offer of which alone would have humiliated him. He pretended to have lost nothing of his gayety, but the forced laughter upon his drawn lips, the quick glance of his eye, still sparkling with fever and excitement, could deceive only the shallowest of friends or minds preoccupied.

One day, when Valerio was crossing one of these dark silent little courts, which served as a passage to the armory, where four persons would hardly meet face to face in broad daylight, he saw, near a damp wall, a man trying to support himself, but who fell from weakness. He drew near, and took him in his arms. But what was his surprise when he recognized in this man, in rags, emaciated with hunger, and whom he had taken for a beggar, his old pupil, Bartolommeo Bozza?

"There are then in Venice," said he, "artists more unfortunate than I."

He made him swallow at once a few drops of wine of Istria, a bottle of which he had in his basket. Then he gave him some figs, which the poor man seized voraciously and devoured without removing the skins. When his hunger was somewhat appeased, he recognized the kindly man who had assisted him. A torrent of tears flowed from his eyes, but Valerio never knew whether it was shame, remorse, or gratitude which caused them; for Bozza did not utter a word, and tried to flee. The gentle Valerio detained him.

"Where are you going, my poor fellow?" said he. "Do you not see that your strength has not returned, and that you will fall in a few minutes a little farther on? I am poor also, and I cannot offer you money, but come with me; your old friends will open their arms to you, and while there is a measure of rice in San Filippo you shall share it with them."

Then he took him by the hand, and Bozza allowed himself to be led mechanically, showing neither joy nor surprise.

XXI.

FRANCESCO could not repress a movement of repugnance when Bozza appeared before him. He knew that this young man, honest in many respects and incapable of a mean action, had no kindness, no affection, no generous impulses in his heart. In him all expressions of tenderness and sympathy were overruled by his indomitable pride and inexorable ambition. However, when Francesco learned in what a condition Valerio had found him, he hastened to find him a pair of shoes and one of his best suits, and offered them to him while his brother prepared for him a substantial meal. From this moment Bozza became one of this poor family, which, by dint of economy, method, and labor, still lived honorably at San Filippo. Valerio did not regret the trouble he had been to, and in the evening, when he saw his old school reunited around the frugal board, his heart beat again with joy, and his whole being was filled with happiness. Then Francesco's restless eyes met those of Bozza, always full of indifference or disdain. Bozza understood nothing of the heroic devotion of the Zuccati. So little conception had he of such nobility of character, that he attributed it to motives of personal interest, to the design of founding a new school in order to secure the labor of their apprentices, or to engage their services beforehand, so that they would not join another school. What his companions justly regarded as sublime was to him simply clever.

But poverty threatened them more and more. The Zuccati were determined to endure the severest privations before calling upon the illustrious masters whose friendship they possessed. Their father's fortune was more than mediocre. His pride had always prevented his receiving any assistance from his sons, who occupied, according to his ideas, such a humiliating position. While they had been prosperous, they had handed over to him a part of their salary; but, in order for him to accept it, Titian had to make him consent to receive it in his name. Now that the Zuccati could no longer assist their father, Titian continued, on his own account, to furnish the old man this allowance, and the grateful sons concealed their want from him, fearing to abuse his generosity.

Fortunately Tintoretto watched over them, although he himself was straitened in circumstances at this time. Art seemed to fall into discredit. The confraternities made but modest votive offerings. They talked of selling all the paintings in the studios in order to distribute the proceeds among the poor workmen of the corporations. The noblemen hid all signs of luxury in the depths of their palaces, in order to avoid any great demands that might be made upon them in behalf of the poorer classes. Nevertheless, Tintoretto still found means to assist his unfortunate friends. Besides finding, unknown to them, many purchasers for their beautiful ornaments, he constantly insisted that the Senate should give them employment. He succeeded finally in proving the need of new repairs in the basilica. Some of the walls in Byzantine mosaics (those still to be seen in St. Mark's) might be preserved, but it would be necessary to remove them entirely, and to replace them by means of new mastic. Other portions were altogether irreparable, and it would be necessary to replace them by new compositions before they all fell to dust, which would incur more expense than one would think. The Senate decreed these works to be done, and voted a sum for the purpose; but they decided that the number of workmen in mosaic should be reduced, and, to put an end to all rivalry, there should be but one head and one school. The head should be he who, after a meeting of all the workmen previously employed, should be judged the most capable by the painters of the commission: his school should be organized at once, not by his own choice according to his sympathy and his family interest, but according to the degree of ability of the other competitors known to the commission. There was to be a grand prize, a second prize, and four minor prizes. The number of masters was limited to six.

The committee was then nominated, and was composed of the painters who had examined the works of the Zuccati and the Bianchini. The meeting was opened, and the subject proposed was a picture in mosaic representing Saint Jerome. When Tintoretto carried these joyful tidings to the Zuccati, he placed in their hands the one hundred ducats which was due them for their year's work, and which he had at last succeeded in obtaining. This unexpected triumph over a destiny so unfortunate and so appalling awoke again both Francesco's and Bozza's failing energy, but in a manner strongly contrasted; for while the young man folded in his arms his brother and his dear apprentices, Bartolommeo, with a yell as harsh and wild as that of a sea-gull, darted out of the studio, and was never seen there again.

The first thing he did was to run to the Bianchini and inform them as to their prospective situation. Bozza felt hatred and contempt for the Bianchini, but he could turn them to account. It was very evident that, either through partiality or justice, the works of Francesco and his pupils would be judged the first at the meeting. The Bianchini were only mechanics, and certainly would not be engaged except in subordinate positions upon the future work of the Republic. On the other hand, Bozza knew that Francesco's weak and sickly condition would not allow him to work. He thought that Valerio would accomplish alone the two efforts demanded of the Zuccati, that even the apprentices might have a hand in them; for the allotted time was short, and the committee would take into consideration the promptitude as well as the knowledge of the contestants. In the bottom of his heart he flattered himself that he could rival all the school. During the last days passed at San Filippo he had closely studied the rules of design, and had sought to master the secrets in color and drawing which Valerio had so candidly and generously imparted to him.

Although hoping to surpass the Zuccati, Bozza was not blind to the difficulty of supplanting Francesco, whose name was already illustrious, while his own was still unknown. It was necessary in order to get rid of him that the Procurators should intimidate the judges by the intrigues and menaces of Melchior. Now the Procurators were in favor of the Bianchini, for they had praised them servilely by telling them that they understood painting and mosaic work much better than Tintoretto or Titian. Determined to fight against the talent of the Zuccati, Bozza had only to secure to himself the influence of the Bianchini. He did so by showing the Bianchini that they could not do without him, because they were entirely ignorant of the rules of design, and that their works would surely be discarded by the committee if they did not abandon the direction of them to him. This insolent pretension did not wound the Bianchini. Money was much dearer to them than praise, and the indifference of the painters toward them at the time of the last examination filled them with misgivings for the future. Therefore they accepted Bozza's offer, and even agreed to give him ten ducats in advance. With half of this sum he hastened at once to buy a beautiful chain, which he sent to the Zuccati, and which Francesco placed upon his brother's neck without knowing whence it came.

THE MASTER MOSAIC-WORKERS.

Everywhere work was vigorously resumed. But Francesco, for the moment reanimated with hope, overrated his strength, and, being stricken down with fever after a few days, was obliged to interrupt his work and watch the progress of his school from his bed.

XXII.

THIS relapse caused Valerio such intense anxiety that he had to give up his work and withdraw from the contest. Francesco's condition was serious, and the mental agony he felt at seeing his masterpiece begun and interrupted augmented still more his physical suffering. This agony was still further increased when Ceccato's wife thoughtlessly told him that, in passing by, she had seen Bozza in the Bianchini's studio. This mark of ingratitude seemed to him so black that he cried with indignation, thus heightening his fever. Valerio, seeing him so worried, pretended that Nina was deceived, and that he should go himself and find out if it were true. He could not really believe in such heartlessness on the part of a workman with whom, in spite of so many grievances, he had shared his last penny. He proceeded to San Fantino, where the Bianchini had their studio, and through the open door he saw Bozza occupied in directing the young Antonio. He requested an interview with him, and,

THE MASTER MOSAIC-WORKERS.

having taken him a short distance away, he earnestly reproved him for his conduct.

"Seeing you go away so hurriedly the other day," said he, "I knew very well that, at the first hope of personal success, your old friends would be strangers to you. I understood very well the egotism of the artist, and my brother tried to excuse it, saying that the thirst for glory is a passion so imperious that everything gives way before it; but between egotism and wickedness, between ingratitude and treachery, there is a chasm which I did not believe you could overleap so lightly. All honor to you, Bartolommeo! You have given me a bitter lesson, and you have made me distrustful of the ennobling influence of benefits."

"Do not speak of benefits, Messer," said Bozza, coldly. "I have not accepted any. You assisted me in the hope that I would become useful to you. For my part, I do not wish to become useful to you, and I have repaid your services by a gift, the value of which far surpasses the amount of expense you have been to on my account."

Saying this, Bozza pointed to the chain which Valerio wore on his neck. As soon as Valerio understood to what he referred, he snatched it so violently that it broke into pieces.

"Is it possible," he exclaimed, choking back the tears of shame and anger, — "is it possible that you have dared to send me a gift?"

"This is done every day," answered Bozza. "I do not deny your kindness in receiving me, and I likewise give you credit for knowing me well enough not to be troubled in regard to the expense you have been to in taking care of me."

"So," said Valerio, holding the chain in his trembling hand, and fixing his eyes ablaze with anger upon Bozza, "you took my studio for a shop, and thought I kept open house by way of speculation? It is thus you appreciate my sacrifices, my devotion to my unfortunate brethren! When, in order to give you time to work, I myself prepared your meals, you looked upon me as your cook!"

"I had no such thought," answered Bozza coldly; "I thought you wanted to enlist an artist whom you considered not without talent, and, in order to free myself and make things even with you, I made you a present. Is n't it customary?"

Valerio, exasperated at these words, threw the chain violently in his face. Bozza was struck near the eye, and the blood ran.

"You will pay me for this insult," said he calmly. "If I control myself here, it is because by one word

I could have ten poniards pointed at your throat. We shall meet elsewhere, I hope."

"Do not doubt it," said Valerio.

And they parted.

On returning home, Valerio met Tintoretto, and told him what had just happened. He also informed him of Francesco's relapse. The master was seriously grieved, but, seeing that discouragement had entered Valerio's soul, he carefully refrained from giving him those ordinary consolations which only aggravate still more the suffering of an ardent temperament. He pretended, on the contrary, to share his doubts regarding the future, and to think Bozza very capable of surpassing him in the contest, and of conducting the school of the Bianchini so well that it would excel that of the Zuccati.

"This is all very discouraging to think of," added he. "Here are these men who know in fact nothing about art; but, thanks to a young man who did not know much more a little while ago, thanks to perseverance and pluck, which often take the place of genius, the most brilliant talent will sink into the shade perhaps, where ignorance, or at least bad taste, will bear the palm. Farewell to art; the days of decadence have come."

"Perhaps this misfortune is not inevitable, my

dear master," said Valerio, roused by this assumed air of dejection. "Thanks to God, the contest is not yet opened, and Bozza has not yet produced his masterpiece."

"I will not conceal from you," replied Tintoretto, "that he has made a very fine beginning. I happened to see it yesterday when passing through San Fantino, and I was surprised at it, for I did not believe Bozza capable of such productions. His pupil, young Antonio, is very apt, and moreover Bartolommeo retouches his work so minutely that no defect is allowed to remain in it. He also directs the two others, and the Bianchini are such servile copyists that, with a good instructor, they are capable of drawing very well by a gift of imitation without understanding drawing."

"But indeed, Master," said Valerio with a troubled look, "you will not give the prize to these charlatans to the detriment of the true disciples of art? Messer Tiziano will not do so either?"

"My dear child, in this contest we are not called upon to judge the men, but the works; and, to make more sure of justice, it is probable that their names will be withheld in the proceedings. Besides, you know it is the custom to pronounce judgment upon a piece of work without having seen the signature.

For this reason it is covered up with a slip of paper before the picture is presented to us. This custom is the symbol of the impartiality which ought to guide our judgment. If Bozza surpasses you, my heart will bleed, but my lips shall speak the truth. If the Bianchini succeed, I shall think that imposture has triumphed over loyalty, vice over virtue; but I am not an Inquisitor, and I have only to judge of pieces of enamel arranged in a given space more or less artistically."

"I know that very well, Master," replied Valerio, a little piqued; "but why do you think that the school of the Zuccati will not force you to give it the palm? It fully intends to do so. Who asks any unlawful indulgence from you? We should not do so, even supposing that we were able to obtain it from you."

"You seem so discouraged, my poor Valerio, and you have such an amount of work to do, that, if your brother does not speedily recover, I tremble indeed at the position in which you now are. Moreover, Francesco being sick, has your school an existence? You are an able master, you are endowed with wonderful facility, and inspiration seems to be beforehand with you. But have you not always turned your back upon glory? Are you not indifferent to the applause of the public? Do you not prefer the intoxication of pleasure, a sort of *dolce far niente* existence, to titles, riches, and praise? You are a man highly gifted, my young master; your intelligence might overcome all things. But I must not deceive you; you are not an artist. You scorn the contest, you disdain the prize, you are too broad-minded to descend into the arena. Bozza, with a hundredth part of your genius, will succeed yet by his ambition, perseverance, and stubborn disposition."

"Master, perhaps you are right," said Valerio, who had listened to this speech like one in a dream. "I thank you for having expressed your fears to me; they are the result of a tender solicitude only too well founded. However, Master, we shall see. Adieu."

Saying this, Valerio, following the custom of the time and the country, kissed the hand of the illustrious master, and lightly crossed the Rialto.

XXIII.

VALERIO threw everybody into commotion on going back to the studio. He walked briskly, spoke loudly, hummed with a disconsolate air the refrain of a merry drinking song, said with an air of tenderness some hard words, broke his tools, made fun of his pupils, and, drawing near to his brother's bed, he embraced him passionately, saying to him with a manner half foolish, half inspired, "Come, be easy, Checo, you will win. You will have the grand prize; we will present a masterpiece for the contest. Come, come, nothing is lost. The Muse has not yet reascended to heaven."

Francesco looked at him in amazement.

"What is the matter with you?" said he. "All that you say is so strange! What has happened? Have you had a quarrel with any one? Have you met the Bianchini?"

"Explain yourself, Master; tell us what has happened," added Marini. "If I may believe some talk I overheard this morning in spite of myself, Bozza's picture is already far advanced, and they say it will be a masterpiece. This is why you are annoyed, my Master; but reassure yourself; our efforts —"

"I, annoyed?" cried Valerio; "and since when was I annoyed if one of my pupils distinguished himself? At what moment of my life have you seen me disturbed or uneasy over the success of an artist? Indeed, I am very envious, am I not?"

"What makes you so touchy, my good master?" said Ceccato. "Which of us ever had such a thought? But tell us, we beg of you, if it is true that Bozza has really done something fine?"

"Without doubt," said Valerio, smiling and suddenly resuming his sweetness and accustomed gayety, "he ought to be able to. I gave him good rules enough. Very well. What is the matter with you then, all of you, that you are so down-hearted? One would think you were so many willows hanging over a dried up cistern. Come, what's the matter there? Has Nina forgotten the dinner? Has the *Procurator-Cassiere* ordered a new barbarism? Come, children, to work! We have not a day to lose,—no, not an hour. Come, come, the tools! the enamel! the boxes! let every one surpass himself, for Bozza does fine things, and it is for us to do still finer ones."

From this moment joy and activity reigned again in the little studio at San Filippo. Francesco seemed to come back to life in finding once more in all these friendly looks a gleam of hope, a ray of holy joy, such as formerly had given birth to the masterpieces in the cupola of St. Mark's. Misgivings had for a moment rested on all these young heads, like a leaden dome above the smiling caryatides, but Valerio had driven it away with his good humor. The immense will power he was exerting was concentrated within; he showed it only by an increase of cheerfulness. But a marked change had taken place in Valerio; he was no longer the same man. If he had not fallen a victim to the allurements of vanity, if he had not become one of those jealous mortals who cannot endure that others should become successful or famous, at least he was religiously devoted to his profession. His character had become serious under the mask of gayety. Misfortune had cruelly tried him in the most sensitive part of his soul, by striking those whom he loved, and proving to him by bitter lessons the advantages of regularity. He also came to understand why Francesco, in spite of his economy and uniform habits, found himself in such straitened circumstances the day after the trial. Discovering in his brother's trunk the receipted bills of his own creditors, Valerio had cried like the prodigal son. Great souls often have great faults, but they overcome them; and this it is which distinguishes them from the vulgar. So from that day, Valerio, even when in the best of circumstances, never again departed from the rules of moderation and simplicity which he had imposed upon himself in the secrecy of his heart. He never spoke a word of this resolution to any one, but he showed his gratitude to Francesco by a life-long devotion, and his steadfastness of soul by morality in spite of all temptation.

Innocent mirth, happiness born of industry, song and laughter, awoke again the slumbering echoes of this little room. The winter was severe, but wood was not lacking, and every one had hereafter a fine sable cloak and a warm velvet doublet. Francesco's strength returned as if by a miracle. Nina regained her freshness and grace, and the expectation of giving birth to another child consoled her for the loss of her first-born. The one who survived the plague grew visibly, and little Marie Robusti, his godmother, often came to the studio of the Zuccati to amuse him. This young and charming girl took a special interest in the work of her young friends, and she was already capable of appreciating its worth.

THE MASTER MOSAIC-WORKERS.

At last the great day arrived, and all the pictures were carried to the sacristy of St. Mark's, where the committee were assembled. Sansovino had been added to the masters previously nominated.

Valerio had done his best, and hope was all aglow in his heart. He came to the meeting with that holy trust which is not incompatible with modesty. He loved art for its own sake, and was happy in that he had successfully expressed his thought, and the injustice of men could not wrest from him this innocent satisfaction. His brother was obviously excited, but without false shame, without hatred, and without jealousy. With his beautiful pale face, his delicate trembling lips, his glance at once timid and proud, he anxiously awaited the masters of the committee. All of them wished to be able to award him the prize; but their attention was diverted by a man so wan, so agitated, so convulsively bowing his salutations, half cringing, half insolent, that they were almost frightened, as one is at the sight of a madman. Soon however, Bozza recovered his self-possession and decorum, but he felt every moment as if he should faint away.

The mosaic-workers waited in an adjoining apartment while the Commission proceeded to examine their works. At the end of an hour, which seemed a century to Bozza, they were summoned, and Tintoretto, advancing to meet them, requested them to sit down in silence. His immovable features expressed to none of them what each wished to discover. The silence could be felt. Their breath came short; their throats swelled, their hearts beat quickly. When they had seated themselves on the bench assigned to them, Titian, being the oldest, placing himself near the pictures which had been arranged in a line along the wall, pronounced in a clear, firm voice the following formula:—

"We, Vecelli called Tiziano, Jacopo Robusti called Tintoretto, Jacopo Sansovino, Jacopo Pistoja, Andrea Schiavone, Paolo Cagliari called Veronese, all master painters approved by the Senate and by the honorable and fraternal corporation of painters, commissioned by the glorious Republic of Venice, and nominated by the venerable Council of Ten, to act as judges of the works presented at this meeting, have, with the help of God, the light of reason, and uprightness of heart, attentively, conscientiously, and impartially examined the said works, and have unanimously declared worthy to be promoted to the first mastership, having the direction of all the other masters herein mentioned, only the author of the picture on which we have inscribed the number one, with the seal of the Commission. This picture, the author of which is unknown to us, faithful that we are to the oath that we have taken not to read the signatures before having pronounced on the merit of the works, will now be presented to your eyes as well as to our own."

At the same time, Tintoretto lifted one of the veils which covered the picture, and removed the slip which concealed the signature. Francesco uttered a cry of joy. The awarded picture was his brother's. Valerio, who in his most sanguine moments had never counted on anything more than the second prize, remained motionless, and dared not allow himself to feel any pleasure save that of seeing his brother's delight.

The second awarded picture was Francesco's, the third, Bozza's. But when Tintoretto, who took pity on his suffering and imagined he could give him great pleasure, turned toward him expecting to see him stand like the others and uncover, he was obliged to call him three times. Bozza remained immovable, his arms crossed upon his breast, his back resting against the wall, his head sunken and hidden on his bosom. A third-rate prize was altogether beneath his notice. His teeth were set so tight, and his knees were so drawn up, that they were almost obliged to carry him out after the meeting.

The last prizes fell to Ceccato, Gian Antonio Bianchini, and Marini. The two other Bianchini failed, but the Republic gave them work later on, when it realized that more than the limited number of mosaic-masters were needed. But their task was assigned them in buildings where they would find themselves neither in contact nor rivalry with the Zuccati, and their hatred was forever reduced to powerlessness.

XXIV.

BEFORE breaking up the meeting, Titian exhorted the young laureates not to imagine that they had arrived at perfection, but to work for a long time yet after the models of the old masters and the cartoons of the painters. "It is in vain," said he, "that the vulgar are moved at the sight of brilliant particles neatly joined together in uncouth representations of religious subjects; it is in vain that prejudiced people deny that mosaic work can attain to the beauty of design of fresco painting. May those among you who realize by what processes they have merited our votes and excelled their competitors persevere in the love of truth and the study of nature. May those who have committed the folly of working without rule and without conviction profit by their failure, and apply themselves seriously to study. It is never too late to abandon a false method and to repair lost time."

He entered into a minute examination of all the works exhibited at the meeting, and brought out their beauties and defects. He dwelt particularly on Bozza's errors, after having given great praise to the beautiful parts of his work. He criticised the face of Saint Jerome for lack of grace in the drawing, and for a certain expression of cruelty which was less becoming to a saint than to a pagan warrior, a conventional color devoid of life, a frigid, almost contemptuous look in the eye. "It is a fine face," added he, "but it is not Saint Jerome."

Titian spoke also of the Bianchini, and tried to soften the bitterness of their defeat by praising their works in certain respects. As it was his custom to make his dose of honey a little stronger than his absinthe, after having approved the mechanical part of their work, he tried also to praise their design; but in the midst of a somewhat hazardous speech he was interrupted by Tintoretto, who pronounced these words, contained in the *procès-verbal:* —

"Io non ho fatto giudizio delle figure, ne della sua bontà, perchè non mi è sta domanda."

At the close of this memorable morning, Titian gave a grand dinner to all the painters of the commission, and to all the mosaic-masters who had received a prize. Little Marie Robusti was there dressed as a sibyl, and Titian that evening made her his model for the sketch of the head of the child

Virgin in the beautiful picture to be seen in the Museum of Venice. Bozza did not appear.

The banquet was superb. They gayly drank to the health of the laureates. Titian noticed with surprise Francesco's face and behavior. He did not understand this total absence of jealousy, such tender, devoted fraternal love in an artist. He knew very well that Francesco was not without ambition, but his heart was more exalted than his genius. Valerio was in raptures over his brother's happiness. Sometimes he was so affected by it as to become melancholy. At dessert, Marie Robusti drank to the health of Titian; and, immediately after, Francesco, rising, lifted his cup, and said with a beaming countenance, "I drink to my master, Valerio Zuccato." The two brothers threw themselves into each other's arms, and mingled their tears.

The good Father Alberto, they say, enjoyed himself a little too much, although he drank only a few drops of Grecian wine, while the convivialists drained full cups. He was so gentle and so sincere that his indiscretion only made him diffusive in his praise and admiration.

The old Zuccato came in at the close of the dinner. He was in a bad humor.

"A thousand thanks, Master," said he to Titian,

who offered him a cup. "How can you expect me to drink on a day like this?"

"Is not this the happiest day of your life, comrade?" replied Titian. "On this account, ought you not to empty a flagon of Samos with your friends?"

"No, Master," replied the old man, "it is not a happy day for me. It binds my sons forever to an ignoble calling, and condemns two first-class geniuses to unworthy works. Great heavens! I do not see that this calls for a toast."

He condescended to bow when his sons drank to his health. Then little Marie came to stroke his silvery beard, begging what she called a pardon for her husband.

"Hey day!" said Zuccato, "does this pleasantry still continue, my pretty child?"

"So much so," answered Tintoretto, smiling, "that I wish to give you a betrothal dinner at the earliest opportunity."

History does not say whether this dinner ever took place, or whether Valerio Zuccato married Marie Robusti. It is to be supposed that they remained intimately united, and that the two families were always one. In vain did Francesco desire to abdicate his authority in virtue of his brother's claims: he was obliged by Valerio's persistency to return to his position as first master, so that Valerio's title remained purely honorary. The school of the Zuccati once more became successful and happy. Nothing was changed, except that Valerio led a regular life, and that Gian Antonio Bianchini, influenced by good example and won by good deeds, became an excellent artist in conduct as well as in ability. Happy days succeeded this new horizon, and the Zuccati produced other masterpieces, a description of which would take too long, and moreover you have, my children, ample leisure to go and admire them in our basilicas. Bozza's Saint Jerome is in the Exchequer, that of Gian Antonio in the sacristy of St. Mark's. That of Zuccato was sent as a gift to the Duke of Savoy. I cannot tell you what has become of it.

HERE ended the Abbé's story. Some allowances must be made for Bozza. In spite of the great failings of this artist, his great sufferings interest us.

"Bozza," said the Abbé, "could not endure the idea of working under the direction of the Zuccati. The dread of finding them still generous after all his faults was more appalling to him than all his punishments. He wandered from city to city, working sometimes at Bologna, sometimes at Padua, living on little and earning still less. In spite of his great talent and his diploma, his haughty manner and gloomy appearance inspired mistrust. He was not over sensitive to poverty, but obscurity was the torment of his life. He returned to Venice after a few years, and the Zuccati obtained a mastership for him and occupation. Times had changed. The government had become less strict in its reforms. Bozza could work; but it seems that Tintoretto could never forgive him for his conduct toward the Zuccati. The stiff old man, obliged to furnish him with cartoons, made him wait so long for them that Bozza, in a letter which we have, complains of being reduced to want by the delays of the master. The Zuccati had nothing of this kind to fear: they could design their own subjects, and moreover they were loved and esteemed by all the masters. They carried the mosaic art to a degree of perfection which has never since been equalled. Bozza has left some beautiful works, but he never could overcome his faults, because his soul was incomplete.

"Marini and Ceccato seem to have outlived the Zuccati, and to have filled their places in the first rank of the mastership.

"And now, my friends," added the Abbé, "if you examine these magnificent walls of mosaic work, accomplished during the period when Venetian painting was at its height, and if you call to mind what I showed you the other day at Torcelli, of some old fragments of Byzantine gypsoplasts, you will see that the destinies of this entirely Oriental art were linked with those of painting until the time of the Zuccati; but later on mosaic work, left to itself, degenerated and finally was lost altogether. Florence seems to have mastered this art, but she uses it solely for decorative purposes. The new chapel of the Medici is remarkable for the richness of the materials employed in its ornamentation. Lapis-lazuli veined with gold, the most precious marbles, ambergris, coral, alabaster, Corsican green, and malachite, are arranged in arabesques and decorative designs with exquisite taste. But our old pictures with their undying colors, our brilliant enamel in all imaginable shades, so ingeniously obtained by the glass manufacturers of Murano, our illustrious mosaic-masters, our rich corporations, and our jovial confraternities exist no longer, except to prove by these monuments, these ruins, or these souvenirs the grandeur of the time which is no more."

Day dawned on the horizon. The gray gulls rose in flocks from the farther extremity of the marshes of Palestrina, and ploughed through the air in all directions, while the light grew visibly brighter every moment. The sun rose with a rapidity of which I was unconscious, and the beauty of that morning threw me into a kind of ecstasy.

"Behold the only thing which strangers cannot

THE MASTER MOSAIC-WORKERS.

take away from us," said the Abbé to me with a sad smile. "If a decree could prevent the sun from rising radiantly on our cupolas, long ago three guardsmen would have signified to it that it should keep its smiles and loving looks for the walls of Vienna."

www.ingramcontent.com/pod-product-compliance
Lightning Source LLC
Chambersburg PA
CBHW021814230426
43669CB00008B/753